Model Accounting AND Financial Policies & Procedures Handbook

FOR NOT-FOR-PROFIT ORGANIZATIONS

BY EDWARD J. McMILLAN, CPA

asae

The author has worked to ensure that all information in this book is accurate as of the time of publication and consistent with standards of good practice in the general management community. As research and practice advance, however, standards may change. For this reason, it is recommended that readers evaluate the applicability of any recommendations in light of particular situations and changing standards.

American Society of Association Executives
1575 Eye Street, N.W.
Washington, DC 20005-1168

Printed in the United States

Library of Congress Cataloging-in-Publication Data

McMillan, Edward J., 1949–
    Model accounting and financial policies and procedures handbook for
not-for-profit organizations / Edward J. McMillan.
      p. cm.
    Includes index.
    ISBN 0-88034-087-8
    1. Nonprofit organizations—Accounting. 2. Nonprofit organizations—Finance.
I. Title.
HF5686.N56M385 1994
    657'.98—dc20
                                          94-20961
                                              CIP

This book is dedicated to the faculty of
Mount Saint Joseph's High School, Baltimore, Maryland.
The education I received at your
hands is invaluable.
Edward "Buddy" McMillan
Class of 1965

Contents

Preface

Protect your organization and yourself by developing an official *Accounting and Financial Policies and Procedures Manual* that is approved by your board of directors.

This guide was written to help you prepare an official *Accounting and Financial Policies and Procedures Manual* for your organization. While the manual discusses and suggests hundreds of financially related subjects and policies, it cannot include every policy that would be appropriate for every organization. Discuss the topics with the appropriate individuals, and use the manual to help you draft customized policies for your organization.

Written procedures will benefit everyone connected with the financial operation of the organization, including the board of directors, the treasurer, the chief executive officer (CEO), the chief financial officer (CFO), and the accounting staff.

The manual reassures your board that the accounting function has formal direction. It describes exactly how organization accounting and financial affairs are to be handled and how the financial statements are to be presented. In addition, a board-approved *Accounting and Financial Policies and Procedures Manual* that has been reviewed by the organization's certified public accounting (CPA) firm will generally satisfy the fiduciary responsibilities of the board and treasurer with regard to financial management oversight.

Generally speaking, the CEO rarely has a formal accounting or financial background but is usually held primarily responsible when financial problems occur. An official *Accounting and Financial Policies and Procedures Manual* assures the CEO that financial affairs are operating in accordance with official board direction. The manual also provides the CEO with a measure of protection against board criticism on how the financial affairs of the organization are being handled.

An official manual assures your financial staff that the financial statements and underlying accounting policies are board approved and directed. As long as the accounting staff is competent and operating effectively, it will generally be isolated from problems concerning financial operation.

The manual should describe the accounting operation and related policies and procedures in clear, simple, and easy-to-understand language. It should clearly state that the organization's staff has no authority to deviate from established organization policy in financial matters.

PREPARING THE MANUAL

You can use the sample policies and procedures manual featured in this book as a guide to help you prepare your own manual. The manual should be written in language that will enable a trained person to understand the organization's financial operation and accounting policies after reviewing it. Your association's manual should do the following:

- Describe the approved method of accounting.
- Illustrate the approved financial statement formats.

- Detail the chart of accounts and the logic behind it.
- List and describe how every account in the statement of activities (income statement) is handled from the accounting and policy perspective.
- List and describe how every account in the statement of financial position (balance sheet) is handled from the accounting and policy perspective.
- Expand the manual to include related financial and internal control policies such as bid requirement policies, check-signing authority, investment policies, and so forth.
- Have the manual reviewed by the organization's independent CPA before it is presented to the board for approval, to ensure the design is in agreement with generally accepted accounting principles as applicable to not-for-profit organizations.

Once the manual has been prepared and adopted, keep it in a loose-leaf binder rather than in a bound format. Accounting procedures, reporting requirements, financial statement formats, and financial terminology change from time to time. A looseleaf format allows you to change only the affected pages.

Finally, to ensure it is current, have the manual reviewed by the organization's independent CPA firm as part of the annual audit procedures.

About the Author

Edward J. McMillan, CPA, is a nationally recognized speaker, writer, and consultant on not-for-profit financial and management topics for association and chamber of commerce executives. Mr. McMillan currently serves as Faculty Chair for Finance for the U.S. Chamber of Commerce's Institute for Organization Management, where he regularly teaches financial and management courses to association and chamber of commerce executives. Formerly the Finance and Membership Director for the American Correctional Association and the Controller of the national office of Associated Builders and Contractors, Mr. McMillan has served more than 17 years in association management. He is a frequent contributor to ASAE publications.

Edward J. McMillan, CPA
P.O. Box 192
Lothian, MD 20711-9502
(301) 627-2733

Internal Financial Statement Formats

Organizations are free to design internal financial statements in any format that suits them. These statements are not to be confused with audited financial statements compiled by independent CPA firms, as the latter have specific formats and terminology promulgated by the Financial Accounting Standards Board of the American Institute of Certified Public Accountants.

Internal financial statements should simply be designed in a format that meets the particular needs of the individual organization. In an effort to avoid confusion and ensure consistency, however, these statements should at least reasonably approximate the appearance of audited financial statements, should use the same terminology in naming the various statements, and so forth.

The internal financial statements are the basis for the organization's chart of accounts and the *Accounting and Financial Policies and Procedures Manual.*

A typical not-for-profit organization's internal financial statements should include, at a minimum, the following:

1. **The Statement of Financial Position**
    (The Balance Sheet)

2. **The Consolidated Statement of Unrestricted Activities**
    (The Income Statement)

3. **The Statement of Unrestricted Activities by Function**
    (The Income Statement by Function)

4. **The Statement of Temporarily Restricted Activities**
    (The Income Statement of Temporarily Restricted Activities)

5. **The Statement of Permanently Restricted Activities**
    (The Income Statement of Permanently Restricted Activities)

6. **The Statement of Changes in Net Assets**
    (The Statement of Changes in Fund Balances)

The internal financial statements may follow the format of the six financial statements presented on the following six pages. Realistically, these statements, with the exception of the statement of financial position, would also include budget figures for the period.

A sample policy for financial statement preparation and distribution is included among the sample policies in the *Model Accounting and Financial Policies and Procedures Manual* section of this handbook.

Statement of Financial Position
(Balance Sheet)
December 31, 19X1 and 19X0

ASSETS	19X1	19X0
Current Assets:		
Cash and Cash Equivalents	$112,150	$110,230
Accounts and Interest Receivable, Net of Allowance for Doubtful Accounts of $20,000	22,050	21,790
Inventories	10,050	10,070
Prepaid Expenses	10,301	7,050
Short-Term Investments	11,000	10,000
Total Current Assets	$165,551	$159,140
Investments:		
Certificates of Deposit	42,000	40,000
Bonds	11,000	11,000
Total Investments	$ 53,000	$ 51,000
Property and Equipment:		
Land	72,000	72,000
Building and Improvements	607,270	604,140
Furniture and Equipment	71,237	61,055
Leasehold Improvements	12,514	10,509
Total Property and Equipment	$763,021	$747,704
Less Accumulated Depreciation & Amortization	–92,515	–82,470
Total Net Property and Equipment	$670,506	$665,234
TOTAL ASSETS	$889,057	$875,374

LIABILITIES AND NET ASSETS	19X1	19X0
Current Liabilities:		
Accounts Payable	$ 60,801	$ 78,137
Accrued Payroll	15,172	13,033
Total Current Liabilities	$ 75,973	$ 91,170
Long-Term Liabilities:		
Mortgage Payable, Less Current Portion	279,408	367,870
Notes Payable, Less Current Portion	107,742	125,524
Total Long-Term Liabilities	$387,150	$493,394
Deferred Revenues:		
Membership Dues	101,888	91,487
Advertising and Exhibits	51,482	50,882
Total Deferred Revenues	$153,370	$142,369
Total Liabilities	$616,493	$726,933
Net Assets:		
Unrestricted Net Assets	$177,562	$ 51,051
Temporarily Restricted Net Assets	45,002	47,390
Permanently Restricted Net Assets	50,000	50,000
Total Net Assets	$272,564	$148,441
TOTAL LIABILITIES AND NET WORTH	$889,057	$875,374

Consolidated Statement of Unrestricted Activities

(Income Statement)
Year Ended December 31, 19X1

	19X1	19X0
Revenues:		
Membership Dues	$ 664,435	$ 604,405
Interest and Investment Income	6,409	5,335
Publication Sales	99,665	90,411
Less Cost-of-Goods Sold	(19,933)	(18,082)
Advertising	150,230	71,446
Conference Registrations	225,173	200,377
Exhibitors	168,587	139,758
Total Revenues	$1,294,566	$1,093,650
Expenses:		
Personnel:		
Salaries, Exempt	$ 109,574	$ 89,536
Salaries, Nonexempt	191,050	167,666
Salaries, Overtime	25,040	20,404
Fringe Benefits	81,416	73,373
Temporary Agency Fees	27,054	12,599
Independent Contractors	19,990	8,450
Total Personnel	$ 454,124	$ 372,028
Professional:		
Auditing	28,000	25,000
Legal Fees	37,555	23,179
Total Professional	$ 65,555	$ 48,179
Printing	312,951	287,088
Postage	74,892	60,583
Supplies	23,590	21,758
Rent	22,000	20,500
Telephone	63,504	59,946
Utilities	48,911	46,511
Mortgage Interest	32,155	33,552
Other Interest	12,598	14,765
Travel:		
Transportation	33,940	29,743
Lodging	26,659	21,566
Meals	22,522	18,747
Total Travel	$ 83,121	$ 70,056
Insurance	19,077	18,670
Miscellaneous	15,577	12,502
Total Expenses	$1,228,055	$1,066,138
Change in Unrestricted Net Assets	$ 66,511	$ 27,512
Unrestricted Net Assets:		
Beginning of Year	$ 51,051	$ 23,539
End of Year	$ 177,562	$ 51,051

Statement of Unrestricted Activities by Function
(Income Statement)
Year Ended December 31, 19X1

	General Administration	Publications	Membership	Newsletter	Conventions	Total
Revenues:						
Membership Dues			$ 664,435			$ 664,435
Interest & Investment Income	$ 6,409					6,409
Publications Sales		$ 99,665				99,665
Less Cost of Goods Sold		(19,933)				(19,933)
Advertising				$ 150,230		150,230
Conference Registrations					$ 225,173	225,173
Exhibitors					168,587	168,587
Total Revenues	$ 6,409	$ 79,732	$ 664,435	$ 150,230	$ 393,760	$ 1,294,566
Expenses:						
Personnel:						
Salaries, Exempt	18,262	21,914	36,524	14,609	18,265	109,574
Salaries, Nonexempt	31,841	38,210	47,625	23,881	49,493	191,050
Salaries, Overtime	5,008	6,260	4,553		9,219	25,040
Fringe Benefits	13,777	16,596	22,175	9,622	19,246	81,416
Temporary Agency Fees	4,058	5,411	6,763	7,305	3,517	27,054
Independent Contractors		12,050		7,940		19,990
Total Personnel	$ 72,946	$ 100,441	$ 117,640	$ 63,357	$ 99,740	$ 454,124
Professional:						
Auditing	5,600	5,600	5,600	5,600	5,600	28,000
Legal Fees	27,555	10,000				37,555
Total Professional	$ 33,155	$ 15,600	$ 5,600	$ 5,600	$ 5,600	$ 65,555
Printing	12,328	53,805	25,411	197,408	23,999	312,951
Postage	3,923	12,086	6,009	47,182	5,692	74,892
Supplies	3,100	4,598	2,099	6,747	7,046	23,590
Rent	4,400	4,400	4,400	4,400	4,400	22,000
Telephone	10,244	10,795	21,430	8,256	12,779	63,504
Utilities	9,782	9,782	9,782	9,782	9,783	48,911
Mortgage Interest	6,431	6,431	6,431	6,431	6,431	32,155
Other Interest	2,520	2,520	2,520	2,520	2,518	12,598
Travel:						
Transportation	5,464	7,040	7,522	3,033	10,881	33,940
Lodging	4,292	5,933	6,305	2,105	8,024	26,659
Meals	3,626	4,004	4,955	1,973	7,964	22,522
Total Travel	$ 13,382	$ 16,977	$ 18,782	$ 7,111	$ 26,869	$ 83,121
Insurance	3,815	3,815	3,815	3,815	3,817	19,077
Miscellaneous	5,057	2,392	5,637	1,292	1,202	15,580
Total Expenses	$ 181,083	$ 243,642	$ 229,556	$ 363,901	$ 209,876	$ 1,228,058
Change in Unrestricted Assets	$(174,674)	$(163,910)	$ 434,879	$(213,671)	$ 183,884	$ 66,508

Statement of Temporarily Restricted Activities
(Income Statement)
Year Ended December 31, 19X1

Revenue:

*Investment Earnings	$ 4,839
Total Revenue	$ 4,839

Expenses:

Administration	$ 5,040
Bank Fees	2,197
Total Expenses	$ 7,237

Change in Temporarily Restricted Net Assets $ (2,398)

Temporarily Restricted Net Assets:

Beginning of Year	$47,390
End of Year	$45,002

---

*The activity noted is the organization's scholarship fund, which is funded by a transfer of investment earnings from the endowment fund.

Statement of Permanently Restricted Activities

(Income Statement)
Year Ended December 31, 19X1

Revenue:	$ 4,839
*Expenses:	−4,839
Change in Permanently Restricted Assets	$ 0
Permanently Restricted Net Assets:	
Beginning of Year	$50,000
End of Year	$50,000

---

*Transferred to Temporarily Restricted Net Assets

Note: This statement accounts for the organization's endowment fund for scholarships. The corpus is permanently restricted and earnings are transferred to temporarily restricted net assets until the scholarships have been awarded.

Statement of Changes in Net Assets

(Statement of Changes in Fund Balances)
Year Ended December 31, 19X1

	Unrestricted	Temporarily Restricted	Permanently Restricted	Total
Revenues	$1,294,566	$ 4,839	$ —	$1,299,405
Expenses	−1,228,055	−7,237	$ —	−1,235,292
Change in Net Assets	$ 66,511	$ (2,398)	$ —	$ 64,113
Net Assets at Beginning of Year	$ 51,051	$47,390	$ 50,000	$ 148,441
Net Assets at End of Year	$ 117,562	$44,992	$ 50,000	$ 212,554

The Chart of Accounts

At the heart of the accounting operation lies the chart of accounts. The chart of accounts is a required supporting document for audit by an independent CPA firm.

A properly constructed and well-thought-out chart of accounts allows a trained accountant to immediately understand the logic of the accounting coding system and account groupings. Additionally, the chart of accounts includes a brief description of each account, but *not* the formal policy concerning the account. The formal policy is included in the *Accounting and Financial Policies and Procedures Manual,* and the chart of accounts is only one part of this manual.

Because a chart of accounts is a continually growing and changing document, it is best maintained in a loose-leaf binder format. This format allows for additions, deletions, and other updates to be formalized and distributed quickly.

A current chart of accounts is necessary to ensure proper account coding, and everyone who has budgetary responsibility or the authority to approve and code expenditures should have a copy of the chart of accounts.

Employees who have been issued a chart of accounts should sign for the document and the document should be retained in the employee's personnel file. The chart should be clearly marked to indicate that it is not to be photocopied or taken from the building without permission, and it should be returned at the termination of employment. Records of who has possession of the chart of accounts should be retained by both the finance department and the personnel office.

Generally, the chart of accounts is divided into six major account groupings:

- assets
- liabilities
- net assets

Statement of Financial Position
(Balance Sheet)

- revenues
- expenses

Statement of Activities
(Income Statement)

- functions or departments of the organization

These groupings are further subdivided into the account groupings that appear on the organization's financial statements. For example, financial statements often include one expense line item called Travel. This one line item, however, may consist of several types of travel expenses such as transportation, lodging, meals, tips, and so forth. While it is important to maintain this type of detail for management and budgetary purposes, it would be unwieldy to have this much detail appear on the financial statements.

Another expense line item would be called Dues Revenues. Typically, an organization will have several types of members, such as professional, student, retired, and corporate, but only one revenue category called Dues Revenue is noted on the financial statements. Again, detail is maintained in subsidiary accounting records, but only totals are used for reporting purposes.

Literally every account, regardless of how small, should be included in the chart of accounts. Each account should reference the major grouping to which it is assigned, the financial statement reference account, the account number, and a brief description of the account.

A sample policy for the chart of accounts is included among the sample policies in the *Accounting and Financial Policies and Procedures Manual* section of this handbook.

Chart of Accounts Issuance Form

Employee Name: _____

I understand that I have been issued a Chart of Accounts of the organization.

I understand that this document is the property of the organization, is confidential, and is not to be photo-copied or taken from the building without written permission of the Chief Financial Officer.

I also understand that this document is to be returned to the personnel office upon termination of my employment.

Employee Signature: Date:

_____   _____

Approval: Chief Financial Officer

Name: _____

Signature: _____

Date: _____

Chart of Accounts

ASSETS

Financial Statement Reference Account: Cash and Cash Equivalents

Acct. No.	Account Name	Description
10001	Business Checking	Noninterest-bearing general disbursement checking account #_____ at _____ bank.
10002	Payroll Checking	Noninterest-bearing payroll checking account #_____ at _____ bank.
10003	Petty Cash Fund	$250 held on hand for small expenditures of less than $25.
10004	Savings Account	Interest-bearing savings account #_____ at _____ bank.
10005	Certificate of Deposit	____% yielding CD #_____ at _____ bank maturing on _____. Interest is paid quarterly on March 31, June 30, September 30, and December 31 in the form of a check.
10006	Certificate of Deposit	____% yielding CD #_____ at _____ institution maturing on _____. Interest is paid at maturity.

Financial Statement Reference Account: Investments

Acct. No.	Account Name	Description
10010	Bond	____% yielding bond #_____ at _____ institution maturing on _____. Interest is paid semiannually on June 30 and December 31 in the form of a check.
10011	Bond	____% yielding bond #_____ at _____ institution maturing on _____. Interest is paid annually on June 30 in the form of a check.
10012	Stock	____ shares of the common stock of _____ institution. Dividends are paid in the form of a check when declared.

Acct. No.	Account Name	Description
10013	Stock	_____ shares of the common stock of _____ institution. Dividends are paid in the form of a check when declared.

Financial Statement Reference Account: Accounts Receivable

Acct. No.	Account Name	Description
10100	A/R, Publication Sales	Receivable due the organization for the sale of all publications.
10101	A/R, Merchandise Sales	Receivable due the organization for the sale of merchandise.
10102	A/R, Advertising	Receivable due the organization for the sale of all advertising.
10103	A/R, Exhibits	Receivable due the organization for the sale of exhibit booths.
10104	A/R, Conference Registration	Receivable due the organization for the sale of advance and on-site conference registrations.
10105	A/R, Seminars	Receivable due the organization for sponsored seminars.
10106	A/R, Employees	Receivable due the organization from employees for payroll advances and travel advances.
10107	A/R, Members	Receivable due the organization from members for travel advances, etc.
10108	A/R, Nonsufficient Funds Checks	Receivable due the organization for checks that failed to clear the bank because of insufficient funds.
10109	A/R, Other	Other receivables due the organization for anything not having its own category.

Financial Statement Reference Account: Allowance for Doubtful Accounts

Acct. No.	Account Name	Description
10150	Allowance for Doubtful Accounts	Estimate of accounts receivables deemed to be uncollectable.

Financial Statement Reference Account: Prepaid Expenses

Acct. No.	Account Name	Description
10200	Prepaid Insurance	Insurance premiums benefitting future periods.
10201	Conference Facility Deposits	Deposits paid to hotels, convention centers, and so forth, to reserve space for future meetings.
10202	Printing Deposits	Amounts paid to printers in advance for magazines and newsletters.
10203	Postage Meter	Postage meter deposits and end-of-month balance.
10204	Prepaid Maintenance	Equipment maintenance contracts benefitting future periods.
10205	Other Prepaid Expenses	Any prepaid expenses not having their own category.

Financial Statement Reference Account: Inventory

Acct. No.	Account Name	Description
10300	Publications	Cost of directories, manuals, and other books held for resale.
10301	Merchandise	Cost of merchandise held for resale, excluding publications.
10302	Other Inventory	Cost of materials held for resale, excluding publications and merchandise.

Financial Statement Reference Account: Land and Buildings

Acct. No.	Account Name	Description
10400	Land, Headquarters	Undepreciable value of the land under and surrounding the headquarters building.
10401	Headquarters Building	Cost and capitalized repairs and improvements of the headquarters building.
10402	Land, Warehouse	Undepreciable value of the land under and surrounding the warehouse.
10403	Warehouse	Cost and capitalized repairs and improvements of the warehouse.

Acct. No.	Account Name	Description
10404	Land, Future Headquarters Site	Undepreciable value of the land purchased for the site of the planned future headquarters site.

Financial Statement Reference Account: Land and Buildings, Accumulated Depreciation

Acct. No.	Account Name	Description
10450	Accumulated Depreciation Headquarters Building	Accumulated depreciation charged against the headquarters building.
10451	Accumulated Depreciation, Warehouse	Accumulated depreciation charged against the warehouse.

Financial Statement Reference Account: Equipment and Leasehold Improvements

Acct. No.	Account Name	Description
10500	Equipment	Capitalized and depreciable equipment, including capitalized repairs and improvements, costing in excess of $500 individually, excluding buildings and land.
10501	Leasehold Improvements	Capitalized and amortizable leasehold improvements to the rental offices costing in excess of $500 individually.

Financial Statement Reference Account:
Equipment and Leasehold Improvements, Accumulated Depreciation, and Amortization

Acct. No.	Account Name	Description
10550	Accumulated Depreciation, Equipment	Accumulated depreciation charged against equipment.
10551	Accumulated Amortization, Leasehold Improvements	Accumulated amortization charged against leasehold improvements.

CLEARING ACCOUNTS

Financial Statement Reference Account:
None, Clearing Accounts Do Not Appear on the Financial Statements

Acct. No.	Account Name	Description
10600	Fringe Benefits Clearing Account	All payroll taxes and employee fringe benefits, including Federal Insurance Contributions Act (FICA) taxes, unemployment taxes, insurance premiums, and pension payments.
10601	Photocopying Clearing Account	All photocopying expenses, including equipment rental, paper purchases, toner, maintenance, and so forth.
10602	Telephone Clearing Account	All telephone charges with the exception of telephone expenses incurred while traveling.
10603	Credit Card Payments Clearing Account	American Express card payments.
10604	Occupancy Payments Clearing Account	Expenses for water, electricity, gas, management fee, janitorial service, real estate taxes, and so forth.
10605	Rent	All rent payments.

LIABILITIES

Financial Statement Reference Account: Accounts Payable

Acct. No.	Account Name	Description
20001	A/P, Vendors	Accrued obligations due the organization's vendors.
20002	A/P, Taxes	Accrued obligations for withholding taxes.
20003	A/P, Payroll and Fringe Benefits	Accrued obligations for payroll and fringe benefits.
20004	A/P, Current Portion of Long-Term Debt	Portion of mortgages and notes payable and due within one year.
20005	Deferred Compensation	Deferred employee wages.
20006	Accrued Annual Leave	Monetary obligation to employees upon termination for unused vacation.
20007	A/P, Other	Any other obligations payable, excluding long-term debt.

Financial Statement Reference Account: Long-Term Debt

Acct. No.	Account Name	Description
20100	Mortgage Payable, Headquarters Building	Mortgage payable to _____ bank, account #_____, on the headquarters building.
20101	Mortgage Payable, Warehouse	Mortgage payable to _____ bank, account #_____, on the warehouse.
20102	Note Payable, Land	Note payable to _____ bank, account #_____, for the future headquarters site.
20103	Note Payable, Equipment	Note payable to _____ for the computer hardware.
20104	Note Payable, Equipment	Note payable to _____ for the telephone system.

Financial Statement Reference Account: Deferred Revenues

Acct. No.	Account Name	Description
20200	Deferred Dues Revenue	Portion of dues received that applies to future periods.
20201	Deferred Advertising Revenue	Portion of advertising revenues for future publications.
20202	Deferred Exhibit Revenue	Portion of exhibit revenues for future conferences.
20203	Deferred Conference Registrations	Registration monies received for future conferences.
20204	Deferred Seminar Registrations	Registration monies received for future seminars.
20205	Other Deferred Revenues	Any other revenues received that apply to future periods.

NET ASSETS

Financial Statement Reference Account: Unrestricted Net Assets

Acct. No.	Account Name	Description
30000	Generally Unrestricted Net Assets	Cumulative result of operations.
30001	Board-Restricted Net Assets—Legal	Board restricted for anticipated legal expenses.
30002	Board-Restricted Net Assets—Other Contingencies	Board restricted for other unbudgeted contingencies.

Financial Statement Reference Account: Temporarily Restricted Net Assets

Acct. No.	Account Name	Description
30100	Scholarship Contributions	Voluntary scholarship contributions from checkoff box on membership brochures.
30101	New Headquarters Site Fundraiser Contributions	Amounts received from fundraiser for new headquarters building site.
30102	Earnings from _____Endowment	Investment earnings from _____ endowment to fund minority scholarships.

Financial Statement Reference Account: Permanently Restricted Net Assets

Acct. No.	Account Name	Description
30200	_____ Endowment	Corpus of _____ endowment, the earnings of which fund minority scholarships.

REVENUES

Financial Statement Reference Account: Dues

Acct. No.	Account Name	Description
40001	Dues, Professional Members	Dues earned from professional memberships.
40002	Dues, Student Members	Dues earned from student memberships.
40003	Dues, Retired Members	Dues earned from retired members.
40004	Dues, Life Members	Dues earned from life memberships.
40005	Dues, Corporate Members	Dues earned from corporate memberships.

Financial Statement Reference Account: Advertising

Acct. No.	Account Name	Description
40010	Magazine Advertising—January	Advertising earned, January issue.
40011	Magazine Advertising—April	Advertising earned, April issue.
40012	Magazine Advertising—July	Advertising earned, July issue.
40013	Magazine Advertising—October	Advertising earned, October issue.
40014	Newsletter Advertising—February/March	Advertising earned, February/March issue.
40015	Newsletter Advertising—May/June	Advertising earned, May/June issue.
40016	Newsletter Advertising—August/September	Advertising earned, August/September issue.
40017	Newsletter Advertising—November/December	Advertising earned, November/December issue.
40018	Directory	Advertising earned, annual directory.

Financial Statement Reference Account: Publication Sales

Acct. No.	Account Name	Description
40100	*Future of the Profession*	Revenues from the sale of the *Future of the Profession* book.
40101	*History of the Profession*	Revenues from the sale of the *History of the Profession* book.

Note: Every publication held for resale should have its own account number for reporting, tracking, ordering, and budgetary purposes.

Financial Statement Reference Account: Cost of Publications Sold

Acct. No.	Account Name	Description
40150	Cost of Publications Sold	A contrarevenue account indicating the organization's actual cost of the publications sold.

Financial Statement Reference Account: Merchandise Sales

Acct. No.	Account Name	Description
40160	Sweatshirts	Revenues from the sale of sweatshirts with logos.

Acct. No.	Account Name	Description
40161	Watches	Revenues from the sale of watches with logos.

Note: As in the case of publications, every item held for resale should have its own account number for reporting, tracking, ordering, and budgetary purposes.

Financial Statement Reference Account: Cost of Merchandise Sold

Acct. No.	Account Name	Description
40162	Cost of Merchandise Sold	A contrarevenue account that indicates the actual cost to the organization of the merchandise sold.

Financial Statement Reference Account: Discounts Taken

Acct. No.	Account Name	Description
40170	Discounts Taken	A contrarevenue account that indicates discounts given to customers who make prompt payments.

Financial Statement Reference Account: Investment Earnings

Acct. No.	Account Name	Description
40200	Interest on Savings	Interest credited to savings account #_____ at _____ bank.
40201	Yield on Certificates of Deposit	Earnings credited to CD #_____ at _____ bank and CD #_____ at _____ bank.
40202	Yield on Bonds	Earnings credited to bond #_____ with _____ and bond #_____ with _____.
40203	Dividends	Dividends paid from _____ stock and _____ stock.

Financial Statement Reference Account: Exhibits

Acct. No.	Account Name	Description
40300	Advance Exhibits	Revenues from advance exhibitor payments.
40301	On-Site Exhibits	Revenues from on-site exhibitor payments.

Financial Statement Reference Account: Conference Registrations

Acct. No.	Account Name	Description
40400	Advance Registrations, Professional Members	Revenues from professional members at advance registration rates.
40401	Advance Registrations, Student Members	Revenues from student members at advance registration rates.
40402	Advance Registrations, Retired Members	Revenues from retired members at advance registration rates.
40403	Advance Registrations, Life Members	Revenues from life members at advance registration rates.
40404	Advance Registrations, Corporate Members	Revenues from corporate members at advance registration rates.
40405	On-Site Registrations, Professional Members	Revenues from professional members at on-site rates.
40406	On-Site Registrations, Student Members	Revenues from student members at on-site rates.
40407	On-Site Registrations, Retired Members	Revenues from retired members at on-site rates.
40408	On-Site Registrations, Life Members	Revenues from life members at on-site rates.
40409	On-Site Registrations, Corporate Members	Revenues from corporate members at on-site rates.

Financial Statement Reference Account: Seminar Registrations

Acct. No.	Account Name	Description
40500	Advance Seminar Registrations, Member Rate	Revenues from advance seminar registrations for members.
40501	On-Site Seminar Registrations, Member Rate	Revenues from on-site seminar registrations for members.
40502	Advance Seminar Registrations, Nonmember Rates	Revenues from advance seminar registrations for nonmembers.
40503	On-Site Seminar Registrations, Nonmember Rate	Revenues from on-site seminar registrations for nonmembers.

Financial Statement Reference Account: Contributions

Acct. No.	Account Name	Description
40600	General Contributions	Contributions from membership form.
40601	Other Contributions	Unsolicited contributions.

Financial Statement Reference Account: Rental Income

Acct. No.	Account Name	Description
40700	Rental Income, Suite 100	Rent received for Suite 100 of headquarters building.
40701	Rental Income, Suite 203	Rent received for Suite 203 of headquarters building.
40702	Rental Income, Warehouse	Rent received for warehouse space rental.

Financial Statement Reference Account: Insurance Program

Acct. No.	Account Name	Description
40800	Insurance Program Income	Revenue received from insurance carriers for policies issued to members.

Financial Statement Reference Account: Sale of Mailing Lists

Acct. No.	Account Name	Description
40850	Mailing List Sales—Member Rate	Sale of mailing lists to members.
40851	Mailing List Sales—Nonmember Rate	Sale of mailing lists to nonmembers.

Financial Statement Reference Account: Other Income

Acct. No.	Account Name	Description
40900	Other Income	Any income from other revenue sources.

EXPENSES

Financial Statement Reference Account: Wages

Acct. No.	Account Name	Description
50000	Salaries, Exempt	Salaries for exempt employees.
50001	Salaries, Nonexempt	Wages for nonexempt employees.
50002	Salaries, Overtime	Overtime paid to nonexempt employees.
50003	Salaries, Commissions	Wages paid to commission employees.
50004	Salaries, Bonuses	Bonuses paid to all employees.

Financial Statement Reference Account: Fringe Benefits

Acct. No.	Account Name	Description
50010	FICA Taxes	Social Security taxes, employer's share.
50011	Federal Unemployment Taxes	Self-explanatory.
50012	State Unemployment Taxes	Self-explanatory.
50013	Pension Payments	Self-explanatory.
50014	Life Insurance	Self-explanatory.
50015	Health Insurance	Self-explanatory.
50016	Long-Term Disability Insurance	Self-explanatory.
50017	Dental Insurance	Self-explanatory.

Financial Statement Reference Account: Temporary Agency Fees

Acct. No.	Account Name	Description
50030	Temporary Agency Fees	All fees paid to temporary employment agencies, including fees charged for hiring employees of temporary agencies.

Financial Statement Reference Account: Subcontract Labor

Acct. No.	Account Name	Description
50035	Subcontract Labor	Amounts paid to individuals qualifying as independent contractors.

Financial Statement Reference Account: Professional Fees

Acct. No.	Account Name	Description
50040	Audit Fees	Fees paid to CPA firms.
50041	Legal Fees	Fees paid to outside legal counsel.
50042	Other Professional Fees	Professional fees other than accounting and legal.

Financial Statement Reference Account: Office Supplies

Acct. No.	Account Name	Description
50045	Office Supplies	Consumable office supplies not qualifying for capitalization.

Financial Statement Reference Account: Advertising and Promotion

Acct. No.	Account Name	Description
50047	Exhibits	Fees paid to exhibit and promote the organization at other organizations' conferences.
50048	Classified Advertising	Fees paid to advertise the organization, its products, and services in newspapers, magazines, and so forth.

Financial Statement Reference Account: Data Processing

Acct. No.	Account Name	Description
50050	Data Processing Maintenance Contract	Hardware maintenance.
50051	Data Processing Supplies	Consumable data processing supplies.
50052	Software Maintenance	Outside software assistance.
50053	Other Data Processing Hardware Repairs	Repairs not covered by maintenance contract.

Financial Statement Reference Account: Photocopying

Acct. No.	Account Name	Description
50055	Photocopy Supplies	Toner, paper, and so forth.
50056	Photocopy Maintenance Contract	Maintenance contract.

Acct. No.	Account Name	Description
50057	Photocopy Repairs	Repairs not covered by maintenance contract.

Financial Statement Reference Account: Rent

Acct. No.	Account Name	Description
50060	Office Rent	Rent on satellite office.

Financial Statement Reference Account: Telephone

Acct. No.	Account Name	Description
50065	Telephone—MCI	MCI telephone bill.
50066	Telephone—Bell Atlantic	Bell Atlantic telephone bill.
50067	Telephone—Company Cars	Company car telephone.
50068	Telephone—Pagers	Pager fees.

Note: Telephone expenses incurred while on travel status are recorded under the Travel-Telephone expense account.

Financial Statement Reference Account: Postage

Acct. No.	Account Name	Description
50070	Postage—Mail Houses	Fees paid to outside mail houses.
50071	Postage—In-House Meter	Postage on in-house postage meter.
50072	Postage—Postal Permits	Self-explanatory.
50073	Postage—U.S. Post Office	Postage paid directly to post office.

Financial Statement Reference Account: Printing and Typesetting

Acct. No.	Account Name	Description
50080	Brochures	Self-explanatory.
50081	Magazine	Self-explanatory.
50082	Newsletter	Self-explanatory.
50083	Envelopes & Letterhead	Self-explanatory.
50084	Other Printing	Printing that does not meet other categories.

Financial Statement Reference Account: Travel

Acct. No.	Account Name	Description
50090	Local Travel	Self-explanatory.
50091	Airline Travel	Self-explanatory.
50092	Train Travel	Self-explanatory
50093	Taxis	Self-explanatory.
50094	Lodging	Self-explanatory.
50095	Meals	Self-explanatory.
50096	Tips	Self-explanatory.
50097	Telephone	Self-explanatory.
50098	Other Travel	Travel expenses not classified elsewhere.

Financial Statement Reference Account: Maintenance Contracts

Acct. No.	Account Name	Description
50100	Maintenance Contracts	Maintenance on office equipment, excluding data processing, telephone, and photocopy equipment.

Financial Statement Reference Account: Insurance

Acct. No.	Account Name	Description
50105	Insurance—General Liability	Self-explanatory.
50106	Insurance—Office Contents	Self-explanatory.
50107	Insurance—Automobiles	Self-explanatory.
50108	Insurance—Data Processing Equipment	Self-explanatory.
50109	Insurance—Officer & Director Errors and Omissions	Self-explanatory.
50110	Insurance—Umbrella Policy	Self-explanatory.
50111	Insurance—Other	Insurance premiums not classified elsewhere.

Financial Statement Reference Account: Interest Expense

Acct. No.	Account Name	Description
50120	Mortgage Interest—Headquarters	Interest on headquarters mortgage.
50121	Mortgage Interest—Warehouse	Interest on warehouse mortgage.
50122	Note Interest—Land	Interest on land note.
50123	Note Interest—Computer	Interest on computer equipment note.
50124	Note Interest—Telephone	Interest on telephone equipment note.
50125	Other Interest	Interest on credit cards, and so forth.

Financial Statement Reference Account: Occupancy

Acct. No.	Account Name	Description
50130	Real Estate Taxes	Self-explanatory.
50131	Janitorial Service	Self-explanatory.
50132	Alarm System	Self-explanatory.
50133	Trash Service	Self-explanatory.
50134	Cleaning Supplies	Self-explanatory.
50135	Other Occupancy Expenses	Any occupancy expense not classified elsewhere.

Financial Statement Reference Account: Utilities

Acct. No.	Account Name	Description
50140	Water Service	Self-explanatory.
50141	Electricity	Self-explanatory.
50142	Other Utilities	Any utility expense not classified elsewhere.

Financial Statement Reference Account: Depreciation

Acct. No.	Account Name	Description
50150	Depreciation—Headquarters Building	Self-explanatory.
50151	Depreciation—Warehouse	Self-explanatory.
50152	Depreciation—Office Equipment	Self-explanatory.

Financial Statement Reference Account: Amortization

Acct. No.	Account Name	Description
50160	Amortization—Leasehold Improvements	Self-explanatory.

Financial Statement Reference Account: Bank Fees

Acct. No.	Account Name	Description
50165	Bank Fees	Bank fees for service charges, credit card fees, and other debit memorandums.

Financial Statement Reference Account: Discounts Lost

Acct. No.	Account Name	Description
50170	Discounts Lost	Additional expenses incurred from failing to take advantage of vendors' prompt payment discounts.

Financial Statement Reference Account: Repairs and Improvements

Acct. No.	Account Name	Description
50180	Repairs and Improvements	Repairs and improvements to property costing less than $1,000 individually.

Financial Statement Reference Account: Miscellaneous Expenses

Acct. No.	Account Name	Description
50190	Miscellaneous Expenses	Any expense not classified elsewhere.

FUNCTIONS

Financial Statement Reference Department: General Administration

Function No.	Description
10	Expenses relating to the executive, finance, reception, and mail room operations of the organization.

Financial Statement Reference Department: Membership

Function No.	Description
11	Expenses relating to servicing, recruiting, and retaining members of the organization.

Financial Statement Reference Department: Magazine

Function No.	Description
12	Expenses relating to producing the magazine and attracting advertising.

Financial Statement Reference Department: Newsletter

Function No.	Description
13	Expenses relating to producing the newsletter and attracting advertising.

Financial Statement Reference Department: Training

Function No.	Description
14	Expenses relating to marketing and managing training seminars.

Financial Statement Reference Department: Conventions

Function No.	Description
15	Expenses relating to marketing and managing the annual convention.

Financial Statement Reference Department: Publication Sales

Function No.	Description
16	Expenses relating to marketing and selling resale publications.

Financial Statement Reference Department: Directory

Function No.	Description
17	Expenses relating to producing and distributing the annual directory and attracting advertising.

Financial Statement Reference Department: Merchandise Sales

Function No.	Description
18	Expenses relating to marketing and selling merchandise other than publications.

Financial Statement Reference Department: Lobbying

Function No.	Description
19	Expenses relating to the organization's lobbying activities.

The Accounting and Financial Policies and Procedures Manual

Once the organization's chart of accounts has been documented, the next step is to decide official accounting policy on every account appearing on the organization's statement of financial position and various statements of activities.

These policies typically do not have the detail of a chart of accounts, but merely state the official accounting policy on each of the accounts noted and, if applicable, state which items are included in the account. The manual should simply note the account and state the policy.

Additionally, the manual should state official policies on subjects that are related to accounting but that do not necessarily appear on various financial statements. The policies included in this section can be extremely important to the organization and should be well thought out and discussed before being implemented.

A good example of a related subject that should be included in the manual is a member's right to inspect the records of the organization. All members, as well as the public at large, have the right to inspect Form 990, but a member's right to inspect other records varies with state law. Obviously, the policy should comply with law; but if an organization wishes to allow additional member access to records, the policy should be very straightforward and clear.

In this example, assuming the policy has been approved by the board, everyone connected with enforcing the policy is somewhat protected from criticism from members who are denied access to certain records. This protection would apply to the board of directors, the chief executive officer, the chief financial officer, the accounting staff, and literally anyone who has been put in a position of having to enforce any policy included in the manual.

The following are samples of written policies and procedures and forms you may want to consider when preparing your association's own accounting and financial policies and procedures manual. Your manual should include a table of contents and an introductory statement. An example of the statement is as follows:

> The accounting and financial policies included in this manual were approved as official policy of the organization at the Board of Directors' meeting held [date].
>
> All members and staff are bound by the policies herein, and any deviation from established policy is prohibited.

SUBJECT: Access to Records by Members

DISCUSSION: A member's right to access and review a not-for-profit organization's records varies by state. Depending on applicable law, members may have the right to inspect minutes, tax returns, accounting records, and so forth. The policy should, at a minimum, comply with prevailing law.

SAMPLE POLICY: It is the policy of the organization to allow members to inspect the following records of the organization:
    IRS Form 990
    Original applications for tax-exempt status
    Audited financial statements
    (List other records as appropriate.)

SUBJECT: Accounting Method

DISCUSSION: Accounting records are maintained on either the accrual basis of accounting, the cash basis of accounting, or a hybrid system.

Accrual accounting recognizes revenues when they are earned and expenses when they are incurred.

Cash accounting recognizes revenues when the cash is received and recognizes expenses when payment has been made.

Hybrid accounting is a mixture of the two.

Organizations are advised to employ the accrual basis of accounting, as the resulting financial statements are usually far more accurate and meaningful than those developed using the other methods.

SAMPLE POLICY: It is the policy of the organization to utilize the accrual basis of accounting that recognizes revenues when they have been earned and expenses when they have been incurred.

SUBJECT: Accounts Payable Accruals

DISCUSSION: If the organization utilizes the accrual basis of accounting, expenses that have been incurred but not yet paid should be recognized on the financial statements.

The relative materiality of the expenses that have been incurred must be addressed, because distribution of the financial statements should not be delayed in the interest of accruing immaterial expenses. The dollar limit of these expenses will vary according to the size of the organization.

SAMPLE POLICY: It is the policy of the organization to accrue unpaid expenses on its financial records if such expenses are in excess of $250 individually.

SUBJECT:

Accounts Receivable Write-Off Procedures and Authority
(Bad Debts Procedures)

DISCUSSION:

An organization should have prudent accounts receivable write-off procedures for several reasons:

1. To ensure write-offs are not premature.

2. To evaluate account receivable collection effectiveness.

3. To ensure credit isn't reissued to poor credit risks.

The policy should ensure that all available means of collection have been exhausted; that mistakes or misunderstandings don't cause the organization to inadvertently write off balances of customers with good credit; that proper approvals are obtained before write-off procedures are initiated; that everyone involved in the collection process is aware of the procedures; and that the policy addresses how to reestablish credit.

SAMPLE POLICY:

It is the policy of the organization to ensure that all available means of collecting accounts receivable (see Collection Procedures Policy) have been exhausted before write-off procedures are initiated. Write-offs are initiated by a completed Accounts Receivable Write-Off Request Form.

If a receivable is deemed uncollectible, the following approvals are required before write-off implementation:

Amount	Individual
$100 or less	Controller and director of the department responsible for the revenue.
In excess of $100	Chief financial officer and director of the department responsible for the revenue.

Once a write-off has been implemented, appropriate individuals in the ordering department are to be advised to ensure further credit is not allowed and to update the master list of bad accounts.

Customers listed as poor credit risks will be extended future credit only if the back debt, plus accrued interest, is paid and the customer has successfully completed a 90-day cash on delivery (COD) probation period.

A listing of all write-offs for the current month should be included with the monthly financial statements for review by all managers.

If write-off procedures have been initiated, the following accounting treatment applies:

1. Invoices written off that are dated during the current year will be treated as a reduction of the appropriate revenue account.

2. Invoices written off that are dated prior to the current year will be treated as bad debt.

Accounts Receivable Write-Off Request Form

Amount $_____   Invoice # _____   Date of Invoice: _____

_____   _____   _____

_____   _____   _____

Customer: _____

_____

_____

Are invoices attached?   Yes _____   No _____

If no invoice is attached, describe goods or services invoiced:

_____

_____

_____

	Yes	No
Have statements been mailed?	____	____
Has telephone contact been made?	____	____

By: _____

Date: _____

Response: _____

_____

	Yes	No
Has the invoice been turned over to the collection department?	____	____
Has the organization's attorney been advised?	____	____

Requested By: Approved By:

    Name: _____   Name: _____

    Signature: _____   Signature: _____

    Date: _____   Date: _____

SUBJECT: Amortization

DISCUSSION: Amortization is similar to depreciation in that it attempts to recognize the expense associated with a major cash outlay over a period of time rather than in one accounting period.

A leasehold improvement is an expenditure that should be amortized. Such an improvement benefits a tenant's enjoyment of occupancy, but the permanent or remaining value of the expenditure remains with the landlord after the lease terminates. A good example is carpet replacement. The tenant pays for the carpeting, a leasehold improvement, but the carpet remains with the landlord after the lease terminates. In this case, the cost of the carpeting will be amortized over the remaining length of the lease term.

SAMPLE POLICY: It is the policy of the organization to individually amortize leasehold improvements exceeding $1,000 over the remaining length of the lease term. Fully amortized leasehold improvements will be taken off the organization's statement of financial position.

See the Capitalization Cutoff Point Policy in this manual.

SUBJECT: Annual Leave Accrual

DISCUSSION: At the end of their fiscal year, organizations must compute the liability of annual leave due employees as of the last day of the business year and must disclose this liability in the financial statements.

Increases in liability should be computed based on historical data available to the organization and should be budgeted for accordingly. Because this liability account will increase and decrease during the year and because of the difficulty in computing this figure at the end of every month, organizations often absorb and budget for this expense in the last month of the year only.

SAMPLE POLICY: In the last month of the year, it is the policy of the organization to budget for and accrue the value of the annual leave liability due employees.

SUBJECT: Annual Leave Payments

DISCUSSION: It is advisable to cap the amount of annual leave paid to terminating employees and to implement a policy whereby unused leave will be lost.

Employees often use unused leave as a sort of "savings account" in order to maximize monies received at termination of employment. Unfortunately, this practice encourages employees to abuse sick leave and personal leave for their own financial benefit and to the financial detriment of the organization.

SAMPLE POLICY:

It is the policy of the organization to allow employees to carry forward no more than _____ unused vacation days into the next year. Unused leave earned in excess of this amount during the year and not used will be lost.

The maximum amount of annual leave paid to a terminating employee will be the amount of leave carried forward into the subsequent year (not to exceed _____ days), plus the amount of accrued but unused leave earned during the year of termination.

SUBJECT:

Bank Reconciliations

DISCUSSION:

It is *extremely* important, in the interest of proper internal control, that bank reconciliations be handled correctly, because these reconciliations are the final line of defense against improper and fraudulent check disbursements.

Regardless of the size of the organization, three rules of thumb regarding bank statements and reconciliations should be included in the policy:

1. Bank statements should be addressed to, opened by, and reviewed by an executive-level person who is *not* involved in accounting or the bank reconciliation process.

2. Bank reconciliations should be conducted in a timely manner by someone who is not a check signer.

3. Voided checks must be documented and accounted for properly. (See the Voided Checks section in this manual).

Distributing bank reconciliations with internal financial statements is becoming increasingly popular.

SAMPLE POLICY:

It is the policy of the organization to address bank statements to the executive vice president, who will do an initial review of checks that cleared during the prior month.

Within 24 hours, the executive vice president will forward the bank statement to the staff accountant responsible for bank reconciliations. This individual cannnot be a check signer. The staff accountant will answer any questions posed by the executive vice president and prepare the bank reconciliation within 48 hours.

The bank reconciliation will be distributed with the internal financial statements and will include documentation of voided checks.

Bank Reconciliation Form

Month of _____

Bank Balance $ _____

Add: Deposits in Transit:

$ _____ $ _____ $ _____

Total Deposits in Transit   + $ _____

Less: Outstanding Checks:

No.	$ Amount	No.	$ Amount
_____	_____	_____	_____
_____	_____	_____	_____
_____	_____	_____	_____
_____	_____	_____	_____
_____	_____	_____	_____
_____	_____	_____	_____

Bank Reconciliation

Completed by: _____   Total Outstanding Checks   − $ _____

Signature: _____   Adjusted Bank Balance   = $ _____

Date: _____

General Ledger Balance $ _____

Reviewed by: _____

Signature: _____   Date: _____

SUBJECT: Bid Requirements

DISCUSSION: Bids should be required for material expenditures to ensure the organization is receiving the best cost for goods and services.

To accomplish this goal, a formal bid requirement policy should be implemented, and it should apply to all material expenditures when the organization has discretion over the vendor chosen.

Bids should be listed and discussed, and completion of a Selection of Vendor Approval Form should be part of the policy.

SAMPLE POLICY: It is the policy of the organization to require bids for the following expenditures:

Printing   Three bids are required for all printing expenditures exceeding $500.

Capital   Three bids are required for all capital purchases ex-
Purchases   ceeding $1,000.

Inventory   Three bids are required for all inventory purchases ex-
Purchase   ceeding $500.

Professional   Professional services, including CPA firms and law firms,
Services   will be evaluated every three years, and requests for proposals will be prepared and sent to qualified firms in the same field.

Other   All other expenses exceeding $500.

The decision to approve a vendor will be made jointly by the department director and the chief executive officer or chief financial officer.

A completed Selection of Vendor Approval Form will be retained in the file of the vendor chosen.

See the Purchase Orders policy in this manual.

Selection of Vendor Approval Form

Describe Goods or Services: _____

_____

_____

Budgeted Amount $_____

Bids Received:

Vendor #1 Name: _____ Amount $ _____

Vendor #2 Name: _____ Amount $ _____

Vendor #3 Name: _____ Amount $ _____

Vendor chosen: _____

Reason vendor was chosen: _____

_____

_____

Approvals:

Department Director: Chief Executive or
                                              Chief Financial Officer:

Name: _____   Name: _____

Signature: _____   Signature: _____

Date: _____   Date: _____

Note: All bids must be attached to this form.

SUBJECT: Board-Designated Funds

DISCUSSION: Board-designated funds are funds earmarked by an organization's board of directors for a specific purpose. These funds are *not* protected from creditor action and should be included in the unrestricted net assets account on the organization's statement of financial position (balance sheet). It is permissible to include a statement regarding board-designated fund activity in the footnotes or other supplemental information to the financial records, but it will have no legal or accounting significance.

An example of a board-designated fund is a board of directors' decision to earmark a certain percentage of a dues increase for legal contingencies. This fund can be accounted for separately in the internal financial statements, but the board's decision to create the fund merely reflects its desire to set aside this money for legal contingencies. The fund is subject to creditor action and should be included with unrestricted net assets on the statement of financial position.

SAMPLE POLICY: It is the policy of the organization to treat board-designated funds as unrestricted net assets on the statement of financial position. A statement of activity for board-designated funds will be included with footnotes to the financial statements as supplemental information.

See the Unrestricted Net Assets section of this manual.

SUBJECT: Bonding of Employees

DISCUSSION: Not only does it make prudent business sense, but often bonding of employees is required by lending institutions, granting agencies, and so forth. The expense of bonding employees who handle checks and cash is minor in relation to the comfort provided in the event of employee dishonesty.

SAMPLE POLICY: It is the policy of the organization to bond all employees involved in the financial functions of the organization.

SUBJECT: Capitalization Cutoff Points

DISCUSSION: The capitalization cutoff point is the dollar figure under which an item is expensed in the period purchased and over which an item is capitalized and depreciated.

When deciding on this figure, the materiality of the item's cost in relation to the budget as a whole must be considered. The larger the organization's budget, the higher this figure can be.

An acceptable range would be from $250 to $1,000.

SAMPLE POLICY: It is the policy of the organization to expense assets in the period purchased if these assets cost $250 or less individually.

Assets costing in excess of $250 individually will be capitalized and depreciated in accordance with the organization's depreciation policies.

Repairs and improvements to real property and leasehold improvements will be capitalized if they cost in excess of $1,000 individually.

SUBJECT:	Chart of Accounts
DISCUSSION:	At the heart of the accounting operation lies the chart of accounts.

The chart of accounts should be constructed to allow a trained accountant an immediate understanding of the accounting numbering system. It should include a brief description of the use of each account.

Generally, a chart of accounts is divided into the following six account groupings:

1. Assets

2. Liabilities

3. Net assets

4. Revenues

5. Expenses

6. Functions or departments of the organization

The numbering system should clearly indicate the account grouping in which the account belongs. For example, all asset accounts begin with the number one, all liability accounts begin with the number two, and so forth.

See the Chart of Accounts section of this handbook.

SAMPLE POLICY:

It is the policy of the organization to maintain a chart of accounts. All employees involved with accounting coding responsibilities or budgetary responsibilities will be issued a chart of accounts, and the chart of accounts must be updated on a routine basis.

Employees who have been issued a chart of accounts will sign a Chart of Accounts Issuance Form, and the chart of accounts will be returned at the termination of employment.

Chart of Accounts Issuance Form

Employee Name: _____

I have been issued the organization's Chart of Accounts.

I understand that this document is the property of the organization, is confidential, and is not to be photocopied or taken from the building without written permission of the chief financial officer.

I also understand that this document is to be returned to the personnel office upon termination of my employment.

Employee Signature: Date:

_____   _____

Approval: Chief Financial Officer

Name: _____

Signature: _____

Date: _____

SUBJECT: Check Disbursements

DISCUSSION: With the exception of small cash expenditures that are handled by petty cash fund disbursements, most other expenditures will be handled by check.

Because of the need for internal control, the policies concerning check disbursements should be very straightforward and clear.

These four rules concerning check disbursements should always be followed:

1. Unused checks should be prenumbered, stored under lock and key, and requested formally.

2. Persons approving invoices and other expense vouchers should never sign the resulting check even if they are check signers.

3. All checks should be signed by two persons.

4. All checks should be computer protected or imprinted using a check bonder machine.

The obvious purpose of these rules is to prevent unauthorized persons from coming into contact with out-of-sequence checks. Collusion would be required on the part of three people on check disbursement improprieties, and check alteration is made more difficult.

SAMPLE POLICY: It is the policy of the organization to keep unused check supplies safeguarded under lock and key. Individuals responsible for preparing checks will request the approximate number needed, sign for the numbered checks received, and return all unused checks at the end of each day. Request for Unused Checks Forms will be completed and retained.

All check disbursements will require approved invoices or expense vouchers and will have a completed Check Request Form attached. The resulting checks will be signed by two persons not requesting the check.

Signed checks that have not been mailed or distributed will be put under lock and key at the end of each day.

Check Request Form

Name: _____

Signature: _____ Date: _____

Purpose of Check: _____

_____

_____

Are invoices or other supporting documentation attached?   Yes _____   No _____

Make check payable to: _____

Address: _____

_____

_____

Approved:

Name: _____

Signature: _____ Date: _____

For Accounting Use Only

Account #	$ Amount	Account #	$ Amount
_____	_____	_____	_____
_____	_____	_____	_____
_____	_____	_____	_____
_____	_____	_____	_____

Accounting Coding Approved: Name: _____

Signature _____ Date _____

Request for Unused Checks

Number of checks requested: _____

Employee Name: _____

Employee Signature: _____

Date: _____

Supervisor Name: _____

Supervisor Signature: _____

Date: _____

Checks Received: Beginning Check   # _____

                       Ending Check   # _____

Checks Returned Unused: Beginning Check   # _____

                       Ending Check   # _____

For Custodian of Unused Checks:

I certify that all checks have been accounted for.

Name: _____

Signature: _____

Date: _____

SUBJECT: Check Endorsement/Stamp

DISCUSSION: To minimize the opportunity for embezzlement or other mishandling of checks, the organization should ensure that incoming checks are endorsed before they are delivered to finance.

The endorsement stamp(s) should spell out the full name of the organization; it should be marked "For Deposit Only" and should note the bank name and account number.

SAMPLE POLICY: It is the policy of the organization to endorse checks with a stamp(s) as follows:

> For Deposit Only
> Full Organization Name
> Bank Name
> Account Number

SUBJECT: Check Signers

DISCUSSION: These three rules should govern the selection of individuals to sign checks:

1. People who prepare checks should *never* be check signers.

2. People who reconcile bank statements should *never* be check signers.

3. People who approve invoices for payment should *never* sign the checks for payment of invoices they approve if they are check signers.

Proper segregation of duties is a must to ensure adequate internal controls for check preparation. If an employee approving an invoice for payment is prohibited from signing the check, if the check is prepared by someone who is not a check signer, and if the check is signed by two other individuals not associated with incurring the debt, then, theoretically, collusion would have to exist among four employees before embezzlement could occur.

A proper check-signer policy combined with policies on bid requirements, the use of check request forms, and the use of purchase orders—plus the retaining of an independent CPA firm to perform an internal control survey in conjunction with the annual audit—will minimize the opportunity for employee dishonesty.

SAMPLE POLICY: It is the policy of the organization to give check-signing authority to the following positions:

    Chief Executive Officer

    Chief Financial Officer

    Department Directors

Checks issued for payment of the organization's debts will require *two* signatures of individuals not associated with incurring the debt.

Additionally, individuals involved with check preparation and bank reconciliations are prohibited from having check-signing authority.

SUBJECT: Clearing Accounts

DISCUSSION: Clearing accounts are temporary accounts used in the interest of accounting expediency. They are used during the month, but are "cleared out" at the end of the month and distributed to various functional expense accounts accordingly. Clearing accounts are temporary and do not appear on the financial statements.

Fringe benefit payments and photocopying expenditures are good examples of clearing accounts. It is common practice to charge all fringe benefits—such as payroll taxes, insurance payments, and pension payments—to one clearing account and to distribute the total to the various functions of the organization prorated against actual salaries charged to the function for the month. It would be impractical and unnecessarily time consuming to accurately charge for fringe benefits as they are paid during the month.

With regard to photocopying expenditures, all related photocopying expenses such as supplies and maintenance are commonly charged to one clearing account and distributed to the functions of the organization at the end of the month, based on auditron readings or some other method of distribution. Charging these expenses accurately during the month would again be very difficult and time consuming.

Organizations should consider handling several other expenses via clearing accounts, such as telephone expenses, utility expenses, and credit card payments.

SAMPLE POLICY: It is the policy of the organization to utilize clearing accounts for fringe benefits expenses, photocopy expenses, telephone expenses, occupancy expenses, credit card payments, and rent payments.

SUBJECT: Collection Procedures

DISCUSSION: One of the greatest challenges to an organization is collecting monies it is owed on a timely basis. The policies concerning mailing an organization's invoices, preparing and mailing statements, and follow-up collection procedures should be formal and adhered to with no deviations.

Collection methods will vary from organization to organization and will be affected by law, type of customer, amount of the receivable, use of collection agencies, use of attorneys, and other important factors.

SAMPLE POLICY:

It is the policy of the organization to complete customer orders and forward an invoice with the merchandise. Invoices for services will be sent immediately following completion of the service.

Thirty (30) days after the date of the original invoice, statements will be mailed to customers accompanied by copies of outstanding invoices.

Forty-five (45) days after the date of the original invoice, an employee will contact the customer via telephone and attempt to collect the amount due. A record will be kept of telephone contacts.

If 60 days have elapsed without payment, the account will be turned over to the organization's collection agency if the amount is $_____ or less. If the debt exceeds this figure, the account will be handled by the organization's attorney.

A Bad Debt Collection Activity Record will be maintained to track telephone calls, collection agency action, and attorney usage concerning the customer.

Bad Debt Collection Activity Record

Customer Name: _____ Address: _____

Customer # : _____ _____

Telephone # : _____ _____

Invoice # $ Amount

_____   _____

_____   _____

_____   _____

_____   _____

Date: _____ Employee Name: _____

Collection Activity: _____

_____

_____

Date: _____ Employee Name: _____

Collection Activity: _____

_____

_____

Date: _____ Employee Name: _____

Collection Activity: _____

_____

_____

SUBJECT: Contract Signing Authority

DISCUSSION: The organization should have a firm policy regarding what individuals have the authority to sign contracts and other instruments obligating the organization; the policy should also state when that authority exists. Typically, the authority to sign contracts is vested with the chief executive officer or the chief financial officer, as long as the financial implications of the contract are included in the organization's budget. Unbudgeted obligations typically require board of directors' approval before authority to sign the contract is granted.

SAMPLE POLICY: It is the policy of the organization to grant authority to sign contracts to the chief executive officer or the chief financial officer, as long as the financial implications of the contract are included in the organization's budget.

                                  If the financial implication of signing a contract is not included in the organization's budget, board of directors' approval is required before authority to sign the contract is granted.

SUBJECT: Contributions

DISCUSSION: As part of the Omnibus Budget Reconciliation Act of 1993, organizations receiving single contributions of $250 or more must provide written substantiation to the contributor for the contribution to be tax deductible. The contributor's cancelled checks are no longer considered adequate documentation.

                                  Although not necessary, organizations should consider sending thank you letters on letterhead for all contributions, regardless of the amount; the letter should indicate the amount contributed.

SAMPLE POLICY: It is the policy of the organization to send thank you letters on the organization's letterhead acknowledging all contributions, regardless of the amount. The letters will indicate the dollar amount contributed.

                                  See the Quid pro quo Contribution section of this manual.

SUBJECT: Control Over Checks and Cash

DISCUSSION: Internal control of incoming checks and cash is just as serious as control over cash disbursements.

                                  All mail, with the exception of confidential mail, should be opened by *two* people who are rotated on an unpredictable basis, and persons opening the mail should have no accounts receivable or income-producing responsibilities.

                                  After the mail has been opened, a log of checks received that day should be completed by the individuals who have opened the mail. The log should simply record the name of the payer, the check number, the date of the check, the amount of the check, and the invoice number, if applicable. The log should be signed by the person(s) completing it.

Checks should be endorsed before they are given to finance. The endorsement stamp should spell out the organization's full name (never use acronyms), the bank name, and the bank account number.

For example:

> For Deposit Only
> Full Organization Name
> Bank Name
> Account Number

Once the mail has been opened, the check log updated, and the checks endorsed, *all* checks and a copy of the log should be given to an authorized person in the finance department. The individual receiving the checks should sign for them on the original log. To prevent the opportunity for employee dishonesty, original checks should *never* be given to individuals responsible for producing income. If nonfinancial employees have a need to see checks, copies should suffice.

Once checks have been delivered to finance, they should be deposited on the next banking day.

Use of a lock box is discussed elsewhere in the manual.

SAMPLE POLICY:

It is the policy of the organization that all incoming mail will be imprinted with a date- and time-received stamp.

Mail will be opened in the presence of two people. Checks received will be noted on the Daily Checks Received Log Form, which will include the date, the name of the payer, the date of the check, the amount of the check, and the invoice number if applicable. Checks will be endorsed before they are given to finance. Once the checks have been recorded and the log signed by both employees, the checks and a copy of the log will be personally delivered to the responsible person in finance, who will sign for checks received. The original Daily Checks Received Log Form will be given to a senior nonfinancial executive and retained until the annual audit. The log copy included with the checks will also be retained until the annual audit. All checks received will be deposited on the next banking day.

Daily Checks Received Log Form

Today's Date: _____

Employees Opening Mail:

Print Name: _____

Signature: _____

Print Name: _____

Signature: _____

Payer	Check Date	Check No.	Check Amt.	Invoice No.
_____	_____	_____	$_____	_____
_____	_____	_____	_____	_____
_____	_____	_____	_____	_____
_____	_____	_____	_____	_____
_____	_____	_____	_____	_____
_____	_____	_____	_____	_____
_____	_____	_____	_____	_____
_____	_____	_____	_____	_____

Total Number of Checks
Received _____

Total Amount of Checks
Received $_____

Finance Representative: Print Name: _____

Signature: _____   Date: _____

SUBJECT:

CPA Firms:
Audited Financial Statements

DISCUSSION:

Audited financial statements issued by CPA firms must be delivered to each member of the board of directors. Ensuring that members receive these statements is the responsibility of the chief executive officer. Contractual agreements might require the chief executive officer to send audited financial statements to other organizations, such as banks, granting agencies, insurance companies, and so forth.

While audited financial statements are proprietary, consider making them available to the entire membership by publishing them whole or in part in one of the organization's publications, typically the newsletter.

Distribution of the audited financial statements to individuals or organizations not entitled by contractual agreement is a matter of organization policy and is generally left to the discretion of the chief executive officer or the chief financial officer.

SAMPLE POLICY:

It is the policy of the organization to direct the chief executive officer to distribute the audited financial statements to the board of directors and to organizations entitled to receive a copy because of contractual agreement. The decision to publish the statements or otherwise make them available to the membership will be made by the board at its meeting following the issuance of the statements.

The authority to distribute the statements to other individuals or firms requesting them will be left to the discretion of the chief executive officer or the chief financial officer.

An Audited Financial Statements Distribution Log will be maintained.

Audited Financial Statements Distribution Log

Copies of the audited financial statements for the fiscal year ended _____ were sent to the following:

Firm/Individual

Name	Address	Reason	Approved By
_____	_____	_____	_____
	_____	_____	
	_____	_____	
_____	_____	_____	_____
	_____	_____	
	_____	_____	
_____	_____	_____	_____
	_____	_____	
	_____	_____	
_____	_____	_____	_____
	_____	_____	
	_____	_____	

SUBJECT:

CPA Firms:
The Engagement Letter

DISCUSSION:

An engagement letter to a CPA firm is required before an audit commences.

The engagement letter should address topics such as capping audit fees; when the audited statements will be available to management; when tax returns are completed; the availability of a partner to present the audited statements and the management letter to the board; the number of copies of the statements that will be provided; and other matters important to management and the board.

The engagement letter might also specify that the CPA firm will be set up on the database to receive all magazines, newsletters, promotional brochures, and all other mailings sent out, and that the firm will be required to retain this material as part of its permanent audit file for future reference and access, if necessary.

SAMPLE POLICY:

It is the policy of the organization to review the draft of the CPA engagement letter before it is signed to ensure it covers matters important to management.

The engagement letter will be reviewed at the board of directors' meeting immediately before the audit commences. Board approval is required before the president, treasurer, chief executive officer, or chief financial officer are given authority to sign the document.

SUBJECT:

CPA Firms:
The Management Letter

DISCUSSION:

As part of their audit procedures, CPAs are required to report to management any concerns that arise during the audit in the areas of internal control, accounting procedures, and general managerial inefficiencies. These problems are documented in the CPA's management letter.

Management letter issues should be discussed with the board by a representative of the CPA firm.

It is the responsibility of the board to direct staff to the appropriate action required to correct management letter issues and to follow up accordingly.

As in the case of audited financial statements, outside individuals often have a right to obtain a copy of the management letter because of contractual obligation. Banks and insurance companies are typical examples. Distribution of the management letter to others requesting it is usually at the discretion of the chief executive officer or the chief financial officer. A CPA management letter distribution log should be maintained as a record of individuals and firms who have received the report.

SAMPLE POLICY:

It is the policy of the organization to discuss the CPA management letter with representatives of the auditing firm and to direct staff as to the appropriate action required to correct deficiencies addressed.

Distribution of the management letter to individuals or firms other than those entitled to a copy by contractual obligation is left to the discretion of the chief executive officer or the chief financial officer.

A CPA Management Letter Distribution Log will be maintained as a record of those receiving a copy of the report.

CPA Management Letter Distribution Log

The CPA Management Letter for the fiscal year ended _____ has been sent to the following:

Firm/Individual

Name	Address	Reason	Approved By
_____	_____	_____	_____
	_____	_____	
	_____	_____	
_____	_____	_____	_____
	_____	_____	
	_____	_____	
_____	_____	_____	_____
	_____	_____	
	_____	_____	
_____	_____	_____	_____
	_____	_____	
	_____	_____	

SECTION THREE

SUBJECT:	CPA Firms: Selection of Firm
DISCUSSION:	The decision to retain a CPA firm is the responsibility of the board of directors.
	While long-term relationships with CPAs and other professionals have their benefits, prudent business practice dictates a periodic evaluation of the level of services and fees of accountants.
	It is also important to remember that accounting and taxation principles for not-for-profit organizations are different from those of commercial organizations, and the CPA firms interviewed and subsequently selected should specialize in auditing and servicing not-for-profit organizations.
SAMPLE POLICY:	It is the policy of the organization to contract with the CPA firm selected to audit the organization for a period not to exceed three years.
	At the end of this period the organization's treasurer, with the assistance of staff, will interview a minimum of five CPA firms specializing in auditing not-for-profit organizations and make a recommendation to the board of directors for final selection. Reawarding the contract for auditing services to the existing auditing firm is acceptable as long as the interview and selection criteria clearly indicate the firm is the most qualified and cost-effective.
	Additionally, the contract awarding the audit to the CPA firm for a three-year period will have a clause allowing the organization to contract with another firm before the end of the contract period if the current firm provides unsatisfactory service or if the financial condition of the organization prohibits the expense of a full audit.

SUBJECT:	Credit Cards
DISCUSSION:	It is common to issue credit cards to elected leaders and certain management staff.
	A policy should be developed to specify which individuals are entitled to credit cards, and those individuals should sign for the credit cards accordingly, agreeing to abide by travel policies, and so forth. Because a delay often exists between receiving the credit card bill and securing the proper approvals, organizations might want to use the clearing account method in the interest of accounting expediency, avoiding interest payments, and so forth.
SAMPLE POLICY:	It is the policy of the organization to issue credit cards to the following individuals:

> Members of the Board of Directors
>
> Committee Chairs
>
> Chief Executive Officer
>
> Chief Financial Officer
>
> Department Directors

Individuals receiving a credit card will sign a Credit Card Issuance Form, and a Credit Card Holders Log will be maintained. Individuals incurring expenses via credit cards will remit a completed Record of Credit Card Transactions.

Credit Card Issuance Form

Name: _____   Title: _____

Credit Card # :   _____

Expiration Date: _____

    I acknowledge receipt of the above-referenced credit card and agree that it is to be used for organization business only. I also agree to abide by established policy regarding travel and other expenses and to submit a timely Monthly Record of Credit Card Transactions accordingly.

Signature: _____

Date: _____

Credit Card Holders Log

Name	Credit Card #	Expiration Date	Issue Date	Return Date
_____	_____	_____	_____	_____
_____	_____	_____	_____	_____
_____	_____	_____	_____	_____
_____	_____	_____	_____	_____
_____	_____	_____	_____	_____
_____	_____	_____	_____	_____
_____	_____	_____	_____	_____
_____	_____	_____	_____	_____
_____	_____	_____	_____	_____
_____	_____	_____	_____	_____
_____	_____	_____	_____	_____
_____	_____	_____	_____	_____
_____	_____	_____	_____	_____
_____	_____	_____	_____	_____
_____	_____	_____	_____	_____
_____	_____	_____	_____	_____
_____	_____	_____	_____	_____
_____	_____	_____	_____	_____
_____	_____	_____	_____	_____

Record of Credit Card Transactions

Name: _____

Month: _____

Date	Merchant Name	Describe Expense	$ Amount		For Accounting Use

Total $ _____

Signature: _____

Date: _____

Approved By:

Name: _____

Signature: _____

Date: _____

SUBJECT: Date- and Time-Received Stamp

DISCUSSION: Organizations can track their effectiveness in processing checks, as well as avoid disagreements with vendors over timeliness of payments and the like, with the use of a date- and time-received stamp on invoices.

This stamp should be imprinted on the *back* of the invoice to avoid disfiguring the face of the invoice. If opening the mail and stamping individual invoices is impractical, then, at a minimum, stamp the back of every envelope, including general correspondence envelopes.

Using a date- and time-received stamp on the back of envelopes is a good practice in general, because it provides proof of date of receipt in the event a delay in the mail causes problems unrelated to accounting.

The back of invoices might also be marked with a date- and time-received-in-accounting stamp. This practice has the advantage of tracking the time it takes accounting to process checks for payment, while protecting the accounting function from criticism in the event of a delay between the invoice's arrival at the organization and its subsequent receipt by accounting for payment.

SAMPLE POLICY: It is the policy of the organization to stamp the back of all envelopes received in the mail with a date- and time-received stamp.

It is also the policy of the organization to attach stamped envelopes to the organization's copy of the invoice as a permanent record of date of receipt.

Additionally, the accounting function will stamp a date- and time-received-in-accounting stamp on the back of each invoice received.

SUBJECT: Deferred Revenues

DISCUSSION: Accrual accounting specifies that revenues will not be recognized on the financial statements until they have been earned. If they have not been earned, they will be detailed and reported as a liability on the financial statements and reported as revenue earned in the proper period.

Confusion exists among nonaccountants as to why deferred revenues are liabilities on the balance sheet. This practice appears contradictory. It can best be explained by example. Suppose an organization is having a conference in December but collects monies from exhibitors and registrants in June. This money should be shown as a liability on the balance sheet as deferred revenues. Why? What would happen, for example, if the facility burned down before the conference was held? The money collected in advance from exhibitors and registrants would have to be refunded! It is a true liability in this case. If the organization had shown this money as revenue earned, it is probable that decisions would have been made on inaccurate data, and the problem would be compounded.

Many revenue sources can be considered as deferred revenue, including, but not limited to, conference receipts, prepaid advertising receipts, advance deposits on unavailable inventory, and so forth.

SAMPLE POLICY:

It is the policy of the organization that revenues that have not been earned will be included with deferred revenues on the financial statements and recorded as revenue when earned.

SUBJECT:

Depreciation

DISCUSSION:

Several depreciation methods are available for use by not-for-profit organizations, such as the following:

1. Modified Accelerated Cost Recover System (MACRS)

2. Straight Line

3. Double Declining Balance

4. Sum of the Year's Digits

5. Income Forecasting

The two most popular methods used by not-for-profit organizations are the straight line method and MACRS.

The majority of not-for-profit organizations use the straight line method if there are no income tax considerations because it is easy, and less depreciation expense is recorded each accounting period.

If there are unrelated business income tax considerations however, MACRS would be appropriate, as it is an accelerated depreciation method. MACRS results in more depreciation expense recorded in each accounting period, creating a lower tax liability.

SAMPLE POLICY:

It is the policy of the organization to depreciate fixed assets other than real property and electronic equipment using the straight line method over a 10-year period.

Real property will be depreciated utilizing the straight line method over a 30-year period.

Electronic equipment will be depreciated using the straight line method over a 5-year period.

Capitalized repairs and improvements will be depreciated using the straight line method based on an analysis of the time the repair or improvement is expected to improve the property.

Fully depreciated fixed assets will remain on the organization's statement of financial position until they are disposed of or otherwise deemed worthless.

Assets will be capitalized in accordance with the organization's capitalization cutoff point policy.

SUBJECT:	Discounts on Accounts Receivable
DISCUSSION:	Organizations often offer discounts to customers if the customers pay before the debts are actually due.
	Typically, it is common to offer a 2% discount if the bill is paid within ten days.
	Effective use of a discount policy can improve cash flow, because many organizations are mandated to take advantage of all discounts.
SAMPLE POLICY:	It is the policy of the organization to offer customers a 2% discount if the invoice is paid within ten days.
	A "Discounts Taken" account, which is a contrarevenue account, will account for these discounts on the financial statements.

Example:

Merchandise Sales		$ XXX
Less Discounts Taken	$ (XXX)	
Less Cost of Goods Sold	(XXX)	(XXX)
Net Merchandise Sales		$ XXX

SUBJECT:	Discounts Lost
DISCUSSION:	Every organization should mandate the taking of vendor discounts and should hold employees responsible for discounts lost as part of the employee's performance record.
	The financial statements should gauge the effectiveness of the policy.
SAMPLE POLICY:	It is the policy of the organization to take advantage of vendor discounts and record the net expense in the financial records.
	If a discount is lost, the amount will be recorded as an expense line item titled Discounts Lost in the financial statements.
	Supervisors of employees guilty of not taking advantage of discounts will be apprised of this violation of policy.

SUBJECT:	Endowment Funds
DISCUSSION:	Endowment funds are included with permanently restricted net assets on the organization's statement of financial position (balance sheet).
	An endowment fund is established when a donor makes a contribution of money (the corpus) or property to an organization and specifies what the endowment and earnings on the endowment are to be used for.
	If set up properly, endowment funds are usually protected from creditor action.

Further discussion on endowment funds can be found in the Permanently Restricted Net Assets section of this handbook.

SAMPLE POLICY:

It is the policy of the organization to include endowment funds with permanently restricted net assets on the organization's statement of financial position.

See the Permanently Restricted Net Assets section of this manual.

SUBJECT:

Federal Identification Number

DISCUSSION:

The Internal Revenue Service is currently pressuring businesses to maintain a record of vendor Federal Identification Numbers (FIN).

In order to save considerable staff time responding to Federal Identification Number requests, many organizations are simply including this number on their invoices, statements, purchase orders, and like documents.

SAMPLE POLICY:

It is the policy of the organization to have the organization's Federal Identification Number printed on its invoices, statements, purchase orders, and any other document that may trigger a customer's request for this information.

SUBJECT:

Financial Statement Preparation and Distribution

DISCUSSION:

Financial statements should be prepared and distributed on a timely basis if the organization is serious about taking a proactive rather than a reactive position in solving problems. If financial statements are not distributed promptly, valuable time that could have been used to correct the problem will be lost.

Financial statements should be prepared and distributed monthly within ten working days after the close of the prior month. The statements should include, at a minimum, the statement of financial position (balance sheet), the statement of activities (income and expense statement), departmentalized or functional statement of activity reports, and other financial reports important to the organization.

Policy should also state who is entitled to a copy of the financial statements.

See the Internal Financial Statement Formats section of this handbook.

SAMPLE POLICY:

It is the policy of the organization to prepare and distribute monthly financial statements that will include the Statement of Financial Position, the Consolidated Statement of Unrestricted Activities, the Statement of Unrestricted Activities by Function, the Statement of Temporarily Restricted Activities, the Statement of Permanently Restricted Activities, and the Statement of Changes in Net Assets. These statements will be prepared and distributed within ten working days after the close of the month.

The statements will be distributed to the board of directors, the budget and finance committee, the chief executive officer, the chief financial officer, and department directors.

SUBJECT: Forms Manual/Retired Forms Manual

DISCUSSION: The organization should maintain an official forms manual for *every* form it uses.

A complete up-to-date forms manual should be issued to every manager; it should be issued to employees on an as-needed basis.

All forms should be reviewed routinely and replaced as needed. Forms should be dated and should include revision dates. Copies of retired forms should be retained permanently in a retired forms manual in the organization's archives.

Consider using customized forms that include the organization's logo. (See Logo section of this manual.) The number of forms used by an organization is, of course, limitless, and depends on the size and shape of the entity.

A suggested sampling of official forms could be as follows:
- Accident Reports
- Bank Reconciliation
- Check Requests
- Daily Checks Received Log
- Daily Lock Box Transaction Log
- Employee Change of Status
- Employee Evaluations
- Employee Reprimands
- Employee Terminations
- Employment Applications
- Envelopes
- Expense Reimbursements
- Inventory Withdrawal Requests
- Invoices
- Letterhead
- Petty Cash Requests
- Purchase Orders
- Receipts Book
- Records Destruction Request
- Requisitions
- Stockroom Withdrawal Requests
- Time Sheets
- Travel Requests

Note: This form schedule is a sample; it is not intended to be all-inclusive.

SAMPLE POLICY: It is the policy of the organization to maintain an official Forms Manual and Retired Forms Manual.

A Forms Manual will be issued to all managers; a manual will be issued to other employees on an as-needed basis.

The Forms Manual will be reviewed and updated on a routine basis as needed.

Retired forms and forms that have been updated or replaced will be retained permanently in the Retired Forms Manual in the organization's archives.

SUBJECT: Fringe Benefits

DISCUSSION: Accounting for the proper allocation of fringe benefits can be very complicated and time consuming.

Organizations can alleviate this situation by using the clearing account method of accounting for fringe benefits and distributing total fringe benefits paid during the month to individual organization functions based on the percentage of salaries charged to each function.

The policy should indicate which expenses are considered fringe benefits and what method is used for allocation.

SAMPLE POLICY: It is the policy of the organization to distribute fringe benefits to the functions of the organization based on actual salaries charged to the functions.

Fringe benefits include FICA taxes, unemployment taxes, employee insurance premiums, and pension payments.

SUBJECT: Independent Contractors

DISCUSSION: It is extremely important to classify employees and independent contractors correctly, as the penalties for noncompliance are severe.

Briefly, the Internal Revenue Service (IRS) has issued a 20-item questionnaire to help employers determine correct employment status. That questionnaire is included with this policy discussion for your reference.

If an individual qualifies for independent contractor status, a contract specifying the agreement should be entered into, and the individual should be sent IRS Form 1099 if compensation is $600 or more.

SAMPLE POLICY: It is the policy of the organization to evaluate criteria established by the IRS when assigning individual employee or independent contractor status. Individuals qualifying as independent contractors will sign an Independent Contractor Agreement and will be issued IRS Form 1099 if compensation is $600 or more.

Independent Contractor Agreement

Name: _____   Social Security #: _____

Address: _____   Home Telephone: _____

_____

_____

I understand that I qualify as an independent contractor under criteria established by the Internal Revenue Service.

As an independent contractor I understand that I am responsible for payment of my own taxes, and employment-related taxes will not be withheld from any payments to me.

I understand that I am not entitled to any employee-related benefits, including, but not limited to, employer's share of FICA taxes, holiday payments, annual or sick leave payments, insurance benefits, unemployment benefits, worker's compensation benefits, and any other benefits of employment not noted.

I understand that by signing this agreement I also agree not to take any future action against the organization with regard to its failing to provide employment benefits that my independent contractor status exempt me from receiving.

For the Organization:

Signature: _____   Name: _____

Date: _____   Signature: _____

Date: _____

Employees versus Independent Contractor's Criteria

Next to each number, write an "E" if employee, "S" if self-employed, or "U" if uncertain.

(1) **Instructions.** A person who is required to comply with instructions about when, where, and how to work is ordinarily an employee.

(2) **Training.** Training of a person by an experienced employee or by other means is a factor of control and indicates that the worker is an employee.

(3) **Integration.** Integration of a person's services into the business operations generally shows that the person is subject to direction and control and accordingly is an employee.

(4) **Services rendered personally.** If the services must be rendered personally by the individual employed, it suggests an employer-employee relationship. Self-employed status is indicated when an individual has the right to hire a substitute without the employer's knowledge.

(5) **Hiring, supervising, and paying assistants.** The hiring, supervising, and paying of assistants by the employer generally indicates that all workers on the job are employees. Self-employed persons generally hire, supervise, and pay their own assistants.

(6) **Continuing relationship.** The existence of a continuing relationship between an individual and the organization for whom the individual performs services is a factor tending to indicate the existence of an employer-employee relationship.

(7) **Set hours of work.** The establishment of set hours of work by the employer is a factor indicating control and accordingly the existence of an employer-employee relationship. Self-employed persons are "masters of their own time."

(8) **Full time required.** If workers must devote full time to the business of the employer, they ordinarily will be employees. A self-employed person on the other hand may choose for whom and when to work.

(9) **Doing work on employer's premises.** Doing the work on the employer's premises may indicate that the worker is an employee, especially if the work could be done elsewhere.

(10) **Order or sequence of work.** If workers must perform services in an order or sequence set by the organization for whom they perform services, it indicates that the workers are employees.

(11) **Oral or written reports.** A requirement that workers submit regular oral or written reports to the employer is indicative of an employer-employee relationship.

(12) **Payment by hour, week, month.** An employee usually is paid by the hour, week, or month, whereas a self-employed person usually is paid by the job on a lump sum basis (although the lump sum may be paid in intervals in some cases).

(13) **Payment of business expenses.** Payment by the employer of the worker's business or travel expenses suggests that the worker is an employee. Self-employed persons usually are paid on a job basis and take care of their own business and travel expenses.

(14) **Furnishing of tools and materials.** The furnishing of tools and materials by the employer indicates an employer-employee relationship. Self-employed persons ordinarily provide their own tools and materials.

(15) **Significant investment.** The furnishing of all necessary facilities (equipment and premises) by the employer suggests that the worker is an employee.

(16) **Realization of profit or loss.** Workers who are in a position to realize a profit or suffer a loss as a result of their services generally are self-employed, while employees ordinarily are not in such a position.

(17) **Working for more than one firm at a time.** A person who works for a number of persons or organizations at the same time is usually self-employed.

(18) **Making services available to the general public.** Workers who make their services available to the general public are usually self-employed. Individuals ordinarily hold their services out to the public by having their own offices and assistants, hanging out a "shingle" in front of their office, holding a business license, and advertising in newspapers and telephone directories.

(19) **Right to discharge.** The right to discharge is an important factor in indicating that the person possessing the right is an employer. Self-employed persons ordinarily cannot be fired as long as they produce results that measure up to their contract specifications.

(20) **Right to terminate.** Employees ordinarily have the right to end the relationship with the employer at any time they wish without incurring liability. A self-employed person usually agrees to complete a specific job and is responsible for its satisfactory completion or is legally obligated to make good for failure to complete the job.

Totals: Employee _____   Self-Employed _____   Uncertain _____

If a genuine question exists as to employment status, it is generally best to side on employee status versus independent contractor status because of the severity of the monetary punishment if found not to be in compliance.

SUBJECT: Insurance

DISCUSSION: In order to protect the organization, employees, and volunteer officers, organizations should have their insurance policies reviewed annually to ensure that coverage and limits are adequate. This review should be conducted by someone trained in commercial insurance who is not the organization's insurance broker.

SAMPLE POLICY: It is the policy of the organization to have an independent insurance consultant review the organization's insurance policies to ensure coverage and limitations adequately meet the needs of the organization, members, and employees.

SUBJECT: Inventory Valuations

DISCUSSION: These are several methods available to value inventory held for resale, and the method chosen should, of course, meet the specific needs of the organization, address tax implications, and so forth. Current methods of inventory valuation include, but are not limited to, the following:

1. Perpetual

2. First-in, First-out (FIFO)

3. Last-in, Last-out (LIFO)

4. Last Cost

5. Average Cost

In addition, other costs besides the actual direct costs of merchandise *can* be included in the calculation of unit cost, such as freight costs, insurance on shipping expenses, and so forth.

SAMPLE POLICY: It is the policy of the organization to use the First-in, First-out (FIFO) method of inventory valuation.

The unit cost will be computed by adding freight costs and insurance on shipping expenses to the actual cost of the inventory, and dividing this dollar amount by the number of units purchased.

SUBJECT: Investment Policy

DISCUSSION: The investment of an organization's excess cash should always be preapproved by the organization's policy-making body. If investment policies are preapproved by the board of directors, executive committee, budget and finance committee, and so forth, the individual(s) making the actual investment decisions will be bound by the policy and prohibited from making risky investment decisions in the hope of achieving a higher investment return than approved investments, no matter how well intended.

Before investments are entered into, an analysis must be done of the cash flow projection budget for the length of time the monies will be obligated. This analysis will ensure that cash is available to meet routine, on-going cash obligations before any investment decisions are made. This analysis will become part of the permanent record surrounding the investment.

Also, the current maximum insured by the Federal Deposit Insurance Corporations (FDIC) is $100,000. This maximum insured amount should be taken into consideration when implementing the investment policy.

SAMPLE POLICY:

It is the policy of the organization to invest excess cash in the following list of approved investments:

Investment Vehicle	Necessary Rating
Certificates of Deposit	(Note Rating)
Bonds	(Note Rating)

The decision to invest cash in approved investments must be made jointly by the chief executive officer and the chief financial officer.

Investment in common stock and other securities not fully insured by the Federal Deposit Insurance Corporation (FDIC) is prohibited.

A completed Investment Authorization Form will be retained with the investment documents.

Investment Authorization Form

Amount: $_____

Describe Investment:

_____

_____

_____

_____

Effective Dates: from _____   to _____

Approved:

Chief Executive Officer: Chief Financial Officer:

Name: _____   Name: _____

Signature: _____   Signature: _____

Date: _____   Date: _____

SUBJECT: IRS Forms:
                                              Form 990

DISCUSSION: Form 990 is an information return required by the IRS of all not-for-
                                              profit organizations with gross revenues of $25,000 or more.

                                              As part of an organization's tax-exempt status, the organization must
                                              make Form 990 available for public inspection, and a firm policy
                                              on this access should be established.

SAMPLE POLICY: It is the policy of the organization to allow public access to IRS
                                              Form 990.

                                              This access will be provided at the organization's headquarters at a
                                              time mutually agreeable between the organization and the individual
                                              requesting the inspection. Requests for copies of Form 990 may be
                                              denied, and Form 990 will not be mailed under any circumstance
                                              without the approval of the chief executive officer or the chief financial
                                              officer. A Log of Form 990 Inspections and Distributions will be maintained.

                                              See the Public and Member Access to Records sections of this manual.

Log of IRS Form 990 Inspections

Fiscal Year Ended _____

Date	Time		Inspector's		Was Copy Provided?		Was Copy Mailed?		Witness/Approval
	From	To	Name	Organization	Yes	No	Yes	No	

SUBJECT:

IRS Forms:
Form 990–T

DISCUSSION:

Form 990–T is a tax return required by the IRS of all not-for-profit organizations with gross unrelated business income tax revenue sources of $1,000 or more.

Since Form 990–T is a tax return, it is considered proprietary information and is not subject to public inspection. Organizations should formalize a policy stating that Form 990–T is confidential and requests to inspect it will be denied.

SAMPLE POLICY:

It is the policy of the organization to deny requests to inspect IRS Form 990–T because it is confidential information.

See the Unrelated Business Income Tax section of this manual.

SUBJECT:

IRS Forms:
Form 1099

DISCUSSION:

IRS regulations require organizations to complete Form 1099 for individuals who are not employees and who receive $600 or more from the organization.

Because of additional requirements for organizations to maintain a record of vendor Federal Identification Numbers, it is becoming increasingly popular to simply issue Form 1099 to all vendors to avoid any potential recordkeeping requirement problems.

At a minimum, a record of vendor Federal Identification Numbers and independent contractor Social Security Numbers should be maintained for audit purposes.

SAMPLE POLICY:

It is the policy of the organization to complete IRS Form 1099 for all individuals and vendors receiving $600 or more from the organization.

A Log of Vendor Federal Identification Numbers will be maintained.

See the Independent Contractors Policy included in this manual.

Log of Vendor Federal Identification Numbers

Vendor Name and Address   Federal Identification #

SUBJECT: Leasehold Improvements

DISCUSSION: Leasehold improvements are capitalized expenditures that improve rental property, but the improvement becomes part of the property after the lease terminates.

A good example of a leasehold improvement is painting. Painting obviously improves rental property, but if the tenant is not reimbursed for this expense, the landlord benefits from the expenditure after the lease terminates.

A policy should be developed regarding what expenditures qualify as leasehold improvements and what the amortization period will be. Typically, a capitalization cutoff point is determined. Expenditures under this amount are considered repairs and expensed when payment is made, and expenditures over this amount are capitalized and amortized over the remaining lease term.

SAMPLE POLICY: It is the policy of the organization to capitalize leasehold improvements costing $1,000 or more. Expenditures under this amount will be considered ordinary repairs and expensed in the period paid. Capitalized leasehold improvements will be amortized over the remaining lease term.

See the Amortization Policy and Repairs and Improvements Policy included in this manual.

SUBJECT: Leases

DISCUSSION: Expensing lease payments in the financial records is based on whether the lease itself is a capital lease or an operating lease.

When an equipment lease is capitalized, the equipment is included among the fixed assets of the organization and depreciated accordingly. Payments for operating leases are considered expenses in the period the lease payment is made.

The decision to classify a lease as a capital lease or an operating lease is technical, and an accountant familiar with the complicated rules used to gauge classification of the lease should be consulted before the decision as to how to record the lease is made.

SAMPLE POLICY: It is the policy of the organization to record leases as either capital leases or operating leases in the financial records, based on appropriate qualification criteria.

SUBJECT:

Loans Prohibited

DISCUSSION:

It is very common for employees to request loans from an organization for emergencies, vacation advances, and the like. Organizations that have granted loans to employees generally regret the practice because it is very difficult to turn down some employees for loans while granting loans to others. However well intentioned, hard feelings between the organization and employees who have been turned down for loans will inevitably surface, and the best course of action is to have a firm policy on prohibiting loans.

SAMPLE POLICY:

It is the policy of the organization to prohibit loans to employees and members under all circumstances.

SUBJECT:

Lobbying Expenditures

DISCUSSION:

As part of the Omnibus Budget Reconciliation Act of 1993, non-501(c)(3) organizations that engage in lobbying activities must either advise their membership of the nondeductible portion of their dues payment or pay the optional proxy tax. In any event, organizations must account for lobbying expenditures, including fees paid to lobbyists, and in-house lobbying expenditures, to the point that they are subject to IRS audit review.

Organizations should have policies that state whether they will advise their membership of the nondeductible portion of their dues payments or pay the optional proxy tax.

SAMPLE POLICY:

It is the policy of the organization to advise members of the nondeductible portion of their dues payments by indicating the nondeductible percentage in the organization's newsletter (annually), in membership brochures, and in membership renewal forms.

or

It is the policy of the organization to pay optional proxy tax on lobbying expenditures.

SUBJECT: Lock Box

DISCUSSION: A lock box is a system whereby incoming checks are mailed directly to and deposited by a bank rather than mailed to the organization.

Use of a lock box is a very effective internal control because employees do not come into contact with original checks and the opportunity for employee dishonesty is virtually eliminated.

A lock box also has several other advantages over mailing checks directly to the organization:

1. Checks are deposited into the organization's account two or more banking days sooner than by traditional methods, so the organization's cash flow and float improves.

2. End-of-month deposits in transit are reduced.

3. Valuable employee time isn't wasted on preparing bank deposits, going to the bank, and so forth.

4. The possibility of losing, misplacing, or having checks stolen is eliminated.

5. Checks are deposited even if employees are out sick, on vacation, and so forth.

When negotiating with the bank, it is suggested that organizations direct the bank to make copies of the original checks and forward the check copies with everything that accompanied the checks, including the envelopes (to record address changes).

Once the lock box receipts are sent to the finance department, accounting *must* balance to the deposit total and record the transaction in the accounting records.

Lock box transactions should be recorded on a daily Lock Box Transaction Log Form and be retained with the bank deposit slip.

SAMPLE POLICY: It is the policy of the organization that checks mailed to the organization be mailed to the lock box at _____ bank.

The bank will copy the checks and forward the copies, deposit slips, and all materials sent with the checks, including the envelopes, to the finance department.

Finance will maintain a Daily Lock Box Transaction Log Form, which will be retained with the bank deposit slips.

Daily Lock Box Transaction Log Form

Deposit Slip Date: _____

Payer	Check Date	Check No.	Check Amount
_____	_____	_____	$_____
_____	_____	_____	_____
_____	_____	_____	_____
_____	_____	_____	_____
_____	_____	_____	_____
_____	_____	_____	_____
_____	_____	_____	_____
_____	_____	_____	_____
_____	_____	_____	_____
_____	_____	_____	_____

Deposit Total $_____

Completed By:

Print Name: _____

Signature: _____

Date: _____

Reviewed By:

Print Name: _____

Signature: _____

Date: _____

SUBJECT: Logo

DISCUSSION: Printing the organization's logo on organization forms such as check requests, purchase orders, expense reimbursement requests, and the like gives the impression that the form is an official form of the organization and not merely a boiler plate copy from another source. In addition, the logo enhances the organization's professional image.

SAMPLE POLICY: It is the policy of the organization to include the organization's logo on all forms used by the organization.

                                See the Forms Manual/Retired Forms Manual section of this manual.

SUBJECT: Long-Term Debt

DISCUSSION: Long-term debt is the amount owed by an organization on mortgages and notes payable that is not due within 12 months. The portion of long-term debt due to be paid within 12 months is considered the current portion of the long-term debt and should be included with the organization's accounts payable on the financial records.

SAMPLE POLICY: It is the policy of the organization to include the current portion of long-term debt (the amount due to be paid within 12 months) with accounts payable on the financial records. Only the noncurrent portion of long-term debts will be included in the long-term debt section of the financial records.

SUBJECT: Monthly Budget Meetings

DISCUSSION: Monthly budget meetings are important if the organization is serious about monitoring revenues, controlling expenses, and ensuring fiscal accountability.

                                Managers should have formal reporting requirements and plans of action to ensure that budgeted goals are met. These monthly budget meetings should be held approximately five working days after the distribution of the monthly financial statements.

                                Monthly financial statements should be prepared and distributed within ten working days after the close of the month.

SAMPLE POLICY: It is the policy of the organization to hold monthly budget meetings within five working days after the distribution of the monthly financial statements. Managers are expected to meet their reporting requirements and report on plans of action to ensure that budgeted goals are met.

SUBJECT: Mailing List Sales

DISCUSSION: The organization has the right to sell its mailing labels/lists/discs, but this policy should be documented and not conflict with prevailing law.

Typically, the sale of membership lists by a not-for-profit organization is permitted as long as the sale is for a product or service that would be of interest to the membership. A differential between the prices charged to members versus nonmembers is also common.

SAMPLE POLICY: It is the policy of the organization to sell membership mailing labels as long as the product or service is of interest to the membership. A discount will apply if the purchaser is a member of the organization.

SUBJECT: Mandatory Vacations/Leave

DISCUSSION: Organizations are urged to implement a financial policy requiring employees to use annual leave.

Requiring the use of annual leave not only caps the amount of leave accrued on the organization's financial statements, but also provides an effective internal control for employees who handle cash and checks.

If employees do not voluntarily take annual leave due them, they should be mandated to take the leave at the employer's discretion.

SAMPLE POLICY: It is the policy of the organization to require employees to take annual leave due them, and no more than _____ vacation days will be carried forward into the next year.

If an employee does not cooperate with this policy, leave will be scheduled at management's discretion. See Leave Accrual Payment Policy in this manual.

SUBJECT: Nonsufficient Funds Checks

DISCUSSION: In the ordinary course of business, checks will occasionally be returned by the bank because of nonsufficient funds on the part of the maker of the checks. These checks can be redeposited if the bank has not altered them by punching holes in the account number on the bottom of the check or has not stamped the check to indicate it may not be redeposited.

When a check is returned because of nonsufficient funds, it should be set up as an account receivable in the accounts receivable, nonsufficient funds account and cash should be reduced accordingly. If the check clears the second time it is deposited, the receivable is reduced.

If the check does not clear on the second try, and the bank alters the check so as to prohibit additional attempts to deposit, then further action is warranted. Generally, the organization will need to contact the maker of the check and request a new check be issued. If this action or any other action fails to rectify the situation, the organization's policy on bad debts would be implemented.

SAMPLE POLICY: It is the policy of the organization to include checks returned by the bank because of nonsufficient funds in the accounts receivable, nonsufficient funds account in the accounting records.

If the checks in question are eligible for redeposit, the subsequent deposit will reduce the receivable account accordingly.

If the checks in question are prohibited from redeposit, the organization's Bad Debts Policy will be implemented.

A Nonsufficient Funds Check Log will be maintained and made available for the annual audit.

Nonsufficient Funds Check Log

Original Deposit Date	Maker of Check	Check #	$ Amount	Membership # or Invoice #	Redeposit Date	Did check clear on redeposit? Yes	No	Was Bad Debt Policy implemented? Yes	No

SUBJECT: Occupancy Expenses

DISCUSSION: Occupancy expenses should be charged to the various functions of the organization on the same basis the organization uses to allocate rent (see discussion on rent in this manual). As in the case of rent, the use of a clearing account to capture occupancy expenses as they are paid during the month is a good idea and is in the interest of both accounting accuracy and payment expediency. If the organization owns its own building, occupancy expenses should be distributed to the various functions of the organization based on the number of people assigned to the function, the amount of square footage assigned to the function, or any other reasonable basis for distribution.

Occupancy expenses typically include real estate taxes, janitorial services, building management fees, utilities (water, gas, and electricity), and so forth.

SAMPLE POLICY: It is the policy of the organization to charge occupancy expenses to the various functions of the organization in accordance with the Rent Distribution Policy addressed elsewhere in this manual.

SUBJECT: Overhead Allocation

DISCUSSION: Although overhead allocations are not required on audited financial statements or by the IRS on Form 990, an organization often distributes overhead expenses to its various functions.

Organizations opting to distribute overhead expenses must first define exactly what expenses constitute overhead expenditures and then allocate these expenses to the various functions of the organization.

Overhead is typically allocated using one of two methods:

1. Direct Cost Basis

2. Direct Salary Basis

SAMPLE POLICY: It is the policy of the organization to allocate overhead expenses to the various functions of the organization on a direct cost basis.

OR

It is the policy of the organization to charge overhead expenses to and include them among the various expense line items of the general administration function.

SUBJECT: Paid Stamp

DISCUSSION: In order to reduce the possibility of paying an invoice twice, organizations should consider altering the invoice with either a "PAID" stamp across the face of the invoice, or use a machine that alters the invoice by punching holes spelling the word "PAID" on the invoice.

An organization can significantly improve the audit trail by including the date paid, the check number, and the check amount.

SAMPLE POLICY:

It is the policy of the organization to alter each invoice with a "PAID" stamp, as follows:

```
┌─────────────────────────┐
│          PAID           │
│  Check # _____   │
│  Date _____    │
│  Check Amt. $_____   │
└─────────────────────────┘
```

SUBJECT:

Permanent Travel Advances

DISCUSSION:

One way to significantly reduce paperwork and check writing for travel advances is to issue employees and members who travel regularly a permanent travel advance.

If, for example, an employee regularly incurs $500 a month in travel expenses, consideration should be given to advancing this amount one time to the employee and reimbursing the employee on a monthly basis. The employee keeps the advance from the time of issuance until termination of employment, when it is deducted from the employee's final payroll check or travel reimbursement check.

This system has several advantages: fewer travel advance checks will have to be issued, fewer petty cash transactions will be required, and required paperwork and check writing will be significantly reduced.

Because the organization has the right to recover the permanent travel advances from the final pay or final travel reimbursement check, this right should be documented and the appropriate form put into the employee's file.

The organization should be prepared to explain this system thoroughly to eligible employees and should not deviate from established policy.

Permanent travel advances should be recorded on the accounting records as a receivable due from employees and should be tracked accordingly.

SAMPLE POLICY:

It is the policy of the organization to issue permanent travel advances to employees who travel on a routine basis.

Employees receiving these advances are instructed not to commingle the advance with their personal funds, as additional travel advances will not be considered. In addition, employees issued permanent travel advances are expected to pay for routine expenses and submit reimbursements for these expenses on a monthly basis rather than request reimbursement from the petty cash fund.

Permanent travel advances will not be deducted from Travel Expense Reimbursement Requests for employees who have been issued a Permanent Travel Advance.

The completed Permanent Travel Advance Issuance Forms will be retained in the affected employees' personnel files.

Permanent Travel Advance Issuance Form

Date: _____

Name of Employee: _____

Advance Amount: $ _____

    I understand that this Permanent Travel Advance has been issued with the understanding that I am expected not to commingle this advance with my personal funds, as additional Travel Advance Requests will not be considered.

    This advance will not be deducted from travel reimbursement requests.

    It is understood that I am prohibited from requesting reimbursement from the petty cash fund, but rather will be reimbursed for these expenses on a monthly basis.

    It is also understood that this advance is a receivable of the organization and it will be deducted from my final paycheck or final expense reimbursement request accordingly.

Signature: _____

Date: _____

Check #_____ was issued on _____ in the amount of $_____ for this advance.

Approval:

Name: _____

Signature: _____

Date: _____

SUBJECT:

Permanently Restricted Net Assets

DISCUSSION:

Permanently restricted net assets are funds designated by the donor to be used for a specific purpose according to the donor's wishes. Permanently restricted net assets are shown on the organization's statement of financial position (balance sheet) and are usually protected from creditor action if handled properly. Proper financial statement presentation dictates that all permanently restricted net assets be added together on the statement of financial position, and a separate statement of activity for permanently restricted net assets be included with the financial statements.

An example of permanently restricted net assets would be an endowment fund. A donor hypothetically contributes a sum of money (the corpus) and stipulates that only the investment earnings of the corpus will be used for a specific purpose—scholarships, for example. The corpus would be considered a permanently restricted net asset, and the investment earnings would be considered a temporarily restricted net asset until the scholarships are awarded.

SAMPLE POLICY:

It is the policy of the organization to add all permanently restricted net assets together for statement of financial position presentation. A separate statement of activity for permanently restricted net assets will be included with the financial statements.

See the Endowment Fund Policy in this manual.

SUBJECT:

Petty Cash Fund Disbursements

DISCUSSION:

In order to reduce check disbursement volume, most organizations maintain a petty cash fund, sometimes called an imprest fund, to pay for small expenditures.

The larger the organization, the larger the petty cash fund can be. Typically, petty cash funds range from $250 to $2,000.

The safeguarding, access to, disbursing, and replenishing of petty cash funds should be very straightforward and clear.

SAMPLE POLICY:

It is the policy of the organization to maintain a petty cash fund of $500.

It is the responsibility of the controller and that person's designee to ensure that the petty cash fund is under lock and key at all times.

Disbursements from the petty cash fund may only be made for approved expenditures. A receipt must accompany every disbursement. The receipt must be signed by the person receiving the cash and the person disbursing the cash.

The petty cash fund will be replenished as needed and at the end of every month. The petty cash fund replenishment check will be made out to the individual primarily responsible for maintaining the fund, with the word "agent" following that person's name. The expenses will be reviewed and the resulting check will be signed by two other responsible parties.

Petty Cash Fund Disbursements Form

Amount: $_____   Date: _____

Purpose: _____

_____

_____

Receipt attached?   Yes _____   No _____

If no receipt, explain: _____

_____

Individual Disbursing Cash:

Name: _____

Signature: _____

Date: _____

Individual Receiving Cash:

Name: _____

Signature: _____

Date: _____

For Accounting Purposes Only

Charge to Account Number: _____

Approved:

Signature: _____

Date: _____

Petty Cash Fund Replenishment and Disbursement Reconciliation Form

Date	$ Amount	Account Number
_____	_____	_____
_____	_____	_____
_____	_____	_____
_____	_____	_____
_____	_____	_____
_____	_____	_____
_____	_____	_____
_____	_____	_____
_____	_____	_____
_____	_____	_____

Total $_____

Note: Completed *Petty Cash Fund Disbursements Forms* and receipts must be attached to the original of this form.

Make check payable to:

_____, Agent.

Approved:

Name: _____

Signature: _____

Date: _____

SUBJECT: Photocopying Expenses

DISCUSSION: The organization should charge the appropriate functions for in-house photocopying expenses based on auditron readings or some other reasonable basis for distribution.

Out-of-house photocopying expenses should, of course, be charged to the function responsible for incurring the expense.

Organizations should use the clearing account method to account for in-house photocopying expenditures.

SAMPLE POLICY: It is the policy of the organization to charge the appropriate functions for in-house photocopying expenses based on auditron readings. A Photocopy Log will be maintained.

Out-of-house photocopying expenses will be charged to the function responsible for incurring the expense.

Photocopy Log

Month: _____

Total Photocopying Expenses Paid: $ _____

Function	Ending Auditron Reading	Beginning Auditron Reading	Copies Made	%	Amount Charged
General Administration					
Membership					
Magazine					
Newsletter					
Training					
Convention					
Directory					
Publication Sales					
Merchandise Sales					
Other:					
					$ _____

Completed By: Name: _____

Signature: _____

Date: _____

SUBJECT: Postage Log

DISCUSSION: Organizations often maintain a postage log to account for in-house postage expenses, typically via a postage meter, and charge the various functions accordingly. Fortunately, most postage meters are relatively sophisticated and can track postage easily.

The log should be set up to account for the beginning postage meter reading, checks issued to increase postage available, and the ending postage meter reading. The actual amount of postage used should equal the amount charged to the functions.

SAMPLE POLICY: It is the policy of the organization to maintain a postage log and to charge the appropriate functions for actual postage used. Employees are prohibited from using the organization's postage meter for personal mail.

Postage Log

Month: _____

Beginning Meter Reading: $_____

Additions:

Attach Postage Meter Tapes to This Form	Date	Check #	$ Amount
	_____	_____	_____
	_____	_____	_____
	_____	_____	_____

Total Additions	+_____
Total Postage Available	$_____
Less Ending Meter Reading	−_____
Total Postage Used	$_____

Function	Postage Used
General Administration	$_____
Membership	_____
Magazine	_____
Newsletter	_____
Seminars	_____
Convention	_____
Publication Sales	_____
Merchandise Sales	_____
Total Postage Used	$_____

Completed By:

Name: _____

Signature: _____

Date: _____

SUBJECT: Prepaid Expenses

DISCUSSION: The payment of expenditures that have future benefits should be detailed and included among the assets of the organization's financial records until expensed in the proper period.

Examples of prepaid expenses include, but are not limited to, insurance premiums, travel expenses to sites of future conferences, room and catering deposits for future conferences, royalty advances, and payment of any expense that has a definite time-sensitive future benefit.

A minimum dollar figure should be established to qualify as a prepaid expense, and *de minimis* payments should be expensed when paid in order to reduce bookkeeping.

Prepaid expenses should be tracked and budgeted for carefully.

SAMPLE POLICY: It is the policy of the organization to treat payments of expenses that have a time-sensitive future benefit as prepaid expenses on the financial records and to expense them in the proper period.

Payment of any expense of $500 or less will not qualify as a prepaid expense.

Records of prepaid expenses will be maintained by the finance department and the originating department and will be budgeted for accordingly.

SUBJECT: Public Access to Records

DISCUSSION: As part of tax exempt status, Form 990 (the organization's annual information return filed with the Internal Revenue Service) is open for public inspection.

Form 990–T, Unrelated Business Income Tax Return, is a tax return, not an information return, and the organization is not obligated to provide this information to the public. Member access is addressed under the Access to Records by Members section of this manual.

SAMPLE POLICY: It is the policy of the organization to allow the public access to Form 990.

This access will be at the organization's headquarters at a mutually agreed upon time.

A responsible employee of the organization will remain in the presence of the individual(s) requesting access to this information. Individuals will be allowed a reasonable amount of time to review the form, but access to copying machines and the like may be denied.

The original of Form 990 will remain at the organization's headquarters without exception.

See Form 990 Policy included in this manual.

SUBJECT:	Purchase Orders
DISCUSSION:	Organizations commonly use a purchase order system to formalize obligations for goods and services and to ensure final senior management approval for expenditures.
	A properly managed purchase order system is effective for controlling expenses, accruing obligations for accounts payable, providing an audit trail when problems occur, and ensuring that disagreements on pricing do not occur.
	Also, organizations often do not extend credit for orders received that are not accompanied by purchase orders.
SAMPLE POLICY:	It is the policy of the organization to use a purchase order system.
	Signed purchase orders will be required for all obligations for goods and services exceeding $500.
	Purchase orders will be prenumbered, kept under lock and key in the finance department, and distributed when an approved Request For Purchase Order has been completed.
	See Bid Requirement Policy.

Request for Purchase Order

Name: _____ Date: _____

Signature: _____

Describe goods or services requested:

_____

_____

Is this item budgeted?   Yes _____   No _____

Has the Bid Requirement Policy been implemented ?   Yes _____   No _____

If *No*, explain: _____

_____

_____

If *Yes*, attach approved Selection of Vendor Approval Form.

Does the cost of this item exceed budget requirements?   Yes _____   No _____

If *Yes*, explain variances:

_____

_____

Approved By:

Name: _____

Signature: _____

Date: _____

Purchase Order

Organization: _____   Date: _____

_____

_____   Purchase Order Number _____

Federal ID # _____

Issued To: _____

_____

_____

_____

Describe goods or services:

_____

_____

_____

Cost: $_____

Approved By:

Name: _____

Signature: _____

Date: _____

SUBJECT: Quid Pro Quo Contributions

DISCUSSION: As part of the Omnibus Budget Reconciliation Act of 1993, organizations must provide written documentation of the deductible portion of quid pro quo contributions in excess of $75.

A quid pro quo contribution is one in which the donor receives a certain amount of value for a contribution—a fundraising dinner, for example, where the donor pays $100 for the ticket, and the meal itself costs the organization $40. In this case the organization must inform the donor that only $60 of the contribution would be deductible as a charitable contribution. Other examples would include auctions, raffles, and so forth.

SAMPLE POLICY: It is the policy of the organization to inform contributors in writing of a good faith estimate of the nondeductible portion of any quid pro quo contributions made for any fundraising activity of the organization if the contribution exceeds $75 individually.

SUBJECT: Records Retention and Destruction

DISCUSSION: Every organization should have a formal, well-thought-out records retention and destruction policy. Old records that are rarely, if ever, used take up valuable, expensive space; yet premature destruction of records can be a costly and sometimes embarrassing mistake.

To address this situation, the organization must first inventory existing records and determine how old they are. After the inventory is complete, a study must be undertaken to determine how long records must be kept, and an appropriate policy established for each type of record eligible for destruction. A formal record of the destruction should be maintained on an permanent basis in a records destruction log. The investigation into how long records must be retained will sometimes uncover inconsistencies among federal, state, and local requirements. When a conflict does exist, the longer period should prevail.

Some records, even though not required by law, should be retained permanently, such as audited financial statements, some personnel records, minutes, legal correspondence, tax records, or other documents that may be important to the organization or eligible for its archives.

SAMPLE POLICY: It is the policy of the organization to retain records as required by law and to destroy them when appropriate.

The destruction of records must be approved via a Records Destruction Request Form. Once the records have been destroyed, a copy of the Records Destruction Request Form will be included in the organization's Records Destruction Log.

The formal records retention policy of the organization is as follows:

Record Retention Period

Accident Reports	_____ Years
Accounting Ledgers Records	_____ Years
Bank Reconciliations	_____ Years
Cancelled Checks	_____ Years
Charts of Accounts	Permanently
Contracts	_____ Years
CPA Audited Financial Statements	Permanently
Depreciation Records	_____ Years
Employee Personnel Records	Permanently
Expense Reimbursements	_____ Years
Insurance Policies	_____ Years
Inventory Records	_____ Years
Invoice Records	_____ Years
Minutes	Permanently
Payroll Records	_____ Years
Petty Cash Records	_____ Years
Purchase Orders	_____ Years
Legal Correspondence	Permanently
General Correspondence	_____ Years
Sales Records	_____ Years
Payment Records	_____ Years
Tax Records	_____ Years

Note: This list is not intended to be all-inclusive.

Records Destruction Request Form

Requesting Employee: _____

Date of Request: _____

Name of Record: _____

Age of Record: _____

Employee Signature: _____

Should this record be microfilmed?   Yes _____   No _____

Method of Destruction: Trash _____   Shredded _____

Has the time requirement for retaining this record been met?   Yes _____   No _____

Approval:

Name: _____   Title: _____

Signature: _____   Date: _____

I certify that this destruction has been completed.

Name: _____   Witness: _____

Signature: _____   Signature: _____

Date: _____   Date: _____

A copy of this form is to be retained by the requesting employee and the original included in the Records Destruction Log.

SUBJECT:	Refunds
DISCUSSION:	Organizations will often receive refund requests from vendors and customers, and a firm refund policy should be in place to assist management.

In the event of dissatisfaction with a product or service, the organization has an obligation to satisfy the customer or member, but within reasonable limits. These limitations should be made clear on order forms, invoices, dues statements, and so forth.

Typically, not-for-profit organizations refund members a pro rata portion of dues paid less a reasonable administrative fee, and full refunds for other goods or services are made if requested within 30 days of the customer's receipt of the invoice requesting payment. Refund payments should reduce the corresponding revenue accordingly.

SAMPLE POLICY: It is the policy of the organization to publish the organization's Refund Policy on order forms, invoices, dues statements, and so forth.

Members requesting a refund for dues will be refunded a pro rata share of unused dues less an administrative fee of $_____.

Full refunds for other goods and services will be granted if the customer or member requests the refund within 30 days of their receipt of the invoice requesting payment.

Refunds issued will reduce the corresponding revenue account accordingly.

SUBJECT: Rent

DISCUSSION: The three most common methods used to allocate rent expense are as follows:

1. Actual square footage occupied by each function

2. Number of employees assigned to individual functions

3. Actual hours spent by employees on various functions per their time sheets

The method chosen should, of course, meet the needs of the individual organization, address unrelated business income tax considerations, and so forth. In any event, adequate documentation is a must for audit purposes.

If the organization does not consistently charge the same amount of rent to individual functions because it subleases offices, charges rent to grant activities, and so forth, it should use the clearing account method to distribute rent expense.

SAMPLE POLICY: It is the policy of the organization to distribute rent expense to the various functions of the organization based on the percentage of employees assigned to that function in relation to the total number of employees of the organization.

SUBJECT: Repairs and Improvements

DISCUSSION: Repairs and improvements to fixed assets or real property will either be expensed in the period paid or capitalized and depreciated if the repair or improvement qualifies for capitalization.

Capitalization of repairs and improvements depends on several factors, including the dollar amount of the expenditure, the remaining useful life of the asset, and whether the asset is owned or leased.

SAMPLE POLICY: It is the policy of the organization to capitalize repairs and improvements to fixed assets or real property owned by the organization if the repairs or improvements cost more than $1,000 individually. Repairs or improvements of $1,000 or less will be expensed in the period paid.

Depreciation of capitalized repairs and improvements will be based on an analysis of how long the repair or improvement is expected to improve or extend the useful life of the property.

See the Capitalization Policy and Leasehold Improvement Policy included in this manual.

SUBJECT: Safe Deposit Box

DISCUSSION: Organizations should rent a safe deposit box from the bank to store securities, original IRS tax-exempt status determination letters, pension approval determination documents, and so forth.

Also, other documents, such as audited financial statements and annual reports, should be permanently stored off-site. Loss of these documents may also mean a loss of any historical perspective of the organization, because recreating the documents may be impossible.

Access to the safe deposit box should be limited to approved check signers and, as in the case of checks, the presence of two persons should be required for access. Two logs should be maintained—a Log of Safe Deposit Box Contents and a Log of Safe Deposit Box Access.

SAMPLE POLICY: It is the policy of the organization to rent a safe deposit box from the organization's bank to store securities, valuables, and important documents such as audited financial statements and annual reports.

Access to the safe deposit box will be limited to check signers, and the presence of two persons is required for access.

A Log of Safe Deposit Box Contents and a Log of Safe Deposit Box Access will be maintained.

Log of Safe Deposit Box Contents

Item Description	Date Stored	Date Removed

Log of Safe Deposit Box Access

Date	Signatures	Reason
_____	_____	_____
	_____	_____
_____	_____	_____
	_____	_____
_____	_____	_____
	_____	_____
_____	_____	_____
	_____	_____
_____	_____	_____
	_____	_____
_____	_____	_____
	_____	_____
_____	_____	_____
	_____	_____

SUBJECT: Salaries and Fringe Benefits Accruals

DISCUSSION: Not-for-profit organizations should accrue unpaid salaries and fringe benefits on their financial statements, because these expenses are typically substantial. Additionally, unpaid wages represent a legal liability to the organization and should be disclosed in the financial statements.

The easiest way to compute this liability is to divide actual salaries paid for the month by the number of work days in the month and multiply this figure by the number of unpaid work days remaining in the month. This calculation should be done by function.

The fringe benefits accrual is computed by multiplying the salary accrual by the appropriate fringe benefits percentage.

SAMPLE POLICY: It is the policy of the organization to accrue unpaid salaries and fringe benefits in the financial statements of the organization, according to function.

SUBJECT: Telephone Expenses

DISCUSSION: Charges for telephone expenses should be allocated to the responsible function based on a review of telephone bills, telephone logs, and so forth.

Organizations often require employees to maintain telephone logs in order to control costs and abuses, and require employees to reimburse the organization for long-distance personal calls.

Organizations should use the clearing account method to account for telephone expenses in the interest of accounting and payment expediency.

SAMPLE POLICY: It is the policy of the organization to require employees to maintain telephone logs to account for all long-distance telephone calls. Employees are required to reimburse the organization for personal telephone calls.

Telephone Log

Employee Name: _____   Telephone Extension: _____

Date	Number Called	Party Called	Was Call Business?	Personal?

Employee Signature: _____   Date: _____

Approved By:

Name: _____   Date: _____

Signature: _____

Charge for Personal Telephone Calls Form

Employee Name: _____ Extension: _____

Telephone logs and bills indicate that you made the following personal long-distance telephone calls:

Date	Telephone Number	$ Cost
_____	_____	_____
_____	_____	_____
_____	_____	_____
_____	_____	_____
_____	_____	_____
_____	_____	_____
_____	_____	_____
_____	_____	_____
_____	_____	_____
_____	_____	_____
_____	_____	_____

Total Cost $_____

The organization has paid this expense on your behalf. You are required to reimburse the organization by check no later than close of business on the next pay date.

Name: _____ Date: _____

Signature: _____

SUBJECT: Temporarily Restricted Net Assets

DISCUSSION: Temporarily restricted net assets are funds received for a designated purpose but that have not been expanded yet. Temporarily restricted net assets are shown on the organization's statement of financial position (balance sheet) and are usually protected from creditor action, if handled properly. Proper financial statement presentation dictates that all temporarily restricted funds be added together on the statement of financial position, and a separate statement of activity for temporarily restricted net assets be included with the financial statements.

An example of a temporarily restricted net asset would be a scholarship fundraiser. The organization appeals for contributions and the monies collected are restricted for the purpose of awarding scholarships and are typically not available to the organization to meet operating expenses. When scholarships are subsequently awarded, the temporarily restricted net asset fund is reduced accordingly, and the expenditure does not appear as a line item expenditure on the organization's financial statements.

SAMPLE POLICY: It is the policy of the organization to add all temporarily restricted net assets together for statement of financial position presentation. A separate Statement of Activity for Temporarily Restricted Net Assets will be included with the financial statements.

SUBJECT: Temporary Employment Agencies

DISCUSSION: Organizations commonly utilize the services of temporary employment agencies to supplement the work force during periods of peak work loads.

Use of temporary employment agencies should require an approval process and records on their use should be maintained for budget purposes and staff evaluation.

Organizations also often hire employees of temporary employment agencies and pay the employment finder's fee. These fees are generally included in the temporary employment agencies line item on the financial statements.

SAMPLE POLICY: It is the policy of the organization to utilize temporary employment agencies to supplement the work force during peak periods. Use of temporary employment agencies requires an approved Request for Temporary Employee Form.

Fees paid to hire the employees of temporary employment agencies are included in the temporary employment agencies line item in the financial statements.

Request For Temporary Employee Form

Agency Requested: _____

_____

_____

Number of Individuals Requested: _____

Length of Time Needed: From _____   To _____

Projected Expense: $_____

Is Expense Budgeted?   Yes _____   No _____

Explain why additional help is requested:

_____

_____

_____

Requesting Employee: Approved By:

Name: _____   Name: _____

Signature: _____   Signature: _____

Date: _____   Date: _____

Function: _____

SUBJECT: Time Sheets

DISCUSSION: The use of time sheets is considered by many to be excessive and unnecessary paperwork. Properly laid-out time sheets, however, are very easy to complete.

Properly completed, signed, and approved time sheets are advantageous to the organization because they provide documentation of every employee's

- actual hours worked;

- overtime hours worked; and

- time off, including
  • administrative leave,
  • holiday leave,
  • vacation leave,
  • sick leave, and
  • leave without pay.

Signed time sheets, with required approvals, can be invaluable to the organization in the event of personnel actions by employees against the organization, audits by local wage and hour authorities, and so forth.

In addition, compensation can be accurately charged to various activities according to actual hours spent working rather than arbitrary time allocations. Accuracy and documentation is important in evaluating budget effectiveness, substantiating expense allocations of unrelated business income tax (in the event of an IRS audit), and so forth.

SAMPLE POLICY: It is the policy of the organization that all employees complete and sign time sheets for every pay period. Paychecks will not be distributed until approved time sheets have been submitted.

Employees will note time spent on various activities in increments of not less than one-half hour.

Employees will note accurately all regular hours, overtime, and leave hours.

Compensation will be charged to the various activities based on a pro rata share of actual hours worked.

TIME SHEET

Employee Name: _____   Employee # : _____   Pay Period Ending: _____

Date: Day:	Sun.	Mon.	Tues.	Wed.	Thurs.	Fri.	Sat.	Accounting: Total Hours	%
Activity: General Admin.									
Membership									
Magazine									
Newsletter									
Training									
Convention									
Directory									
Publn. Sales									
Mdse. Sales									
Total Hours Worked									
Leave Hours: Annual									
Sick									
Holiday									
Without Pay									
Total Leave Hours									
Total Hours									

Employee Signature: _____   Date: _____   Supervisor's Signature: _____   Date: _____

SUBJECT: Travel Advances

DISCUSSION: It is common practice for organizations to issue travel advances to employees and members traveling on organization business.

Organizations should utilize a travel advance request form to monitor the amount of the travel advance and should limit the advance to a predetermined percentage of the estimated expenses.

The travel advance itself is considered an account receivable due from the employee, and the proper travel expense accounts are charged when the final travel expense reimbursement form is turned in for payment at the completion of the travel.

SAMPLE POLICY: It is the policy of the organization to issue travel advances to individuals who have secured the proper travel authorization and have completed a Travel Advance Request Form.

These advances are considered account receivables from the individuals, and the proper travel accounts are charged when reimbursements for travel expenses are paid.

Travel advances are limited to ____% of estimated total travel expenses.

See the Travel Expense Policy and the Permanent Travel Advance Policy included in this manual.

Travel Advance Request Form

Name: _____

Signature: _____

Date: _____

Location to be visited: _____

Purpose of trip: _____

_____

Date: From _____   To _____
                    (day & time)   (day & time)

Estimated Expenses:

Airfare	$_____		Lodging	$_____
Train	_____		Meals	_____
Private Auto	_____		Taxi	_____
Parking	_____		Tips	_____
Rental Car	_____		Telephone	_____
Other	_____	(Detail on reverse)		

Total Estimated Expenses: $_____

Maximum Advance   x_____%

Advance Amount $_____

Approval:

Name: _____

Signature: _____

Date: _____

SUBJECT: Travel Expenses

DISCUSSION: Travel expense reimbursement is one of the most critical areas to control. Effective control requires that formal travel expense forms and travel policy be communicated to the traveler to avoid excessive expense, embarrassment, hard feelings, and general misunderstandings concerning eligible expenses and expense limitations.

                                  Eligible expenses and expense limitations are, of course, dependent on the organization. However frugal or flamboyant, they should be formalized to avoid problems.

SAMPLE POLICY: It is the policy of the organization to establish travel expense limitations and guidelines as follows:

                                  Authorizations — All travel requests must be for budgeted travel and approved at least 30 days in advance by the appropriate manager.

                                  Travel Advances — Travel advances will be issued if requested at least 30 days before the trip. The advance will not exceed _____% of the estimated costs. Travel advances will not be granted to employees who have been issued a permanent travel advance.

                                  Personal Mileage — Employees will be reimbursed for use of their personal cars on organization business at a rate of _____¢ per mile. Commuting mileage will not be reimbursed.

                                  Public Carrier — Employees traveling by public carrier must purchase their tickets from the _____ travel agency. The most cost-effective means of travel, such as coach airfare, must be used without prior written approval of the appropriate manager. Receipts are necessary.

                                  Lodging — Lodging facilities must be approved by the appropriate manager. Employees will be reimbursed entirely for the basic room charge and applicable taxes. Receipts are necessary.

                                  Meals — Employees will be on a per diem basis for meals and tips. Current per diem rates are as follows:

                                  $_____ Breakfast

                                  $_____ Lunch

                                  $_____ Dinner

                                  These figures include applicable taxes.

                                  Receipts are necessary for meals. Tips should be noted on meal receipts.

                                  Taxi — Actual taxi fares, including tips, will be reimbursed entirely. Receipts are necessary. Tips must be noted on taxi receipts.

                                  Telephone — Personal calls must be limited to 15 minutes per day to be reimbursable.

                                  Entertainment — One in-room movie will be reimbursed; all other entertainment expenses must be approved by the appropriate manager to be reimbursable.

Tips — Reasonable tips for baggage handling will be reimbursed. Receipts are not required.

Tips for meals and taxis are discussed elsewhere under these guidelines.

Parking and Tolls — Parking fees and toll expenses will be reimbursed. Receipts are necessary.

Car Rentals — Car rentals will be reimbursed if approved in advance. Receipts are required.

Travel expense reimbursements will be distributed or mailed within 30 days of the finance department's receipt of properly approved requests.

See the Travel Advance Policy and Permanent Travel Advance Policy included in this manual.

Travel Authorization Request Form

Date: _____

Name of Employee: _____ Signature: _____

Location Visited: _____

Dates of Travel: From _____ To _____
  (day & time)   (day & time)

Purpose of trip: _____

_____

Estimated Expenses:

Public Carrier	$_____
Private Automobile	_____
Lodging	_____
Meals	_____
Car Rental	_____
Tips	_____
Entertainment	_____
Taxi	_____
Telephone	_____
Parking & Tolls	_____
Other Expenses (Explain on reverse)	_____
Total Expenses	$_____

If a travel advance is requested, attach a completed Travel Advance Request Form.

Approval:

Name: _____

Signature: _____

Date: _____

Travel Advance Request Form

Name: _____

Signature: _____

Date: _____

Location to be visited: _____

Purpose of trip: _____

_____

Date: From _____   To _____
                    (day & time)   (day & time)

Estimated Expenses:

Airfare	$_____	Lodging	$_____
Train	_____	Meals	_____
Private Auto	_____	Taxi	_____
Parking	_____	Tips	_____
Rental Car	_____	Telephone	_____
Other	_____	(Detail on reverse)	

Total Estimated Expenses: $_____

Maximum Advance   x_____%

Advance Amount $_____

Approval:

Name: _____

Signature: _____

Date: _____

Travel Expense Reimbursement Request Form

Date: _____

Name of Employee: _____ Signature: _____

Location Visited: _____

Dates of Travel: From _____   To _____
                          (date & time)   (date & time)

Expenses: Public Carrier $_____ (Receipt required)

                   Private Automobile   _____ ____ miles at ____¢

                   Lodging   _____ (Receipt required)

                   Meals   _____ (Detail on reverse)

                   Car Rental   _____ (Receipt required)

                   Tips   _____ (Detail on reverse)

                   Entertainment   _____ (Detail on reverse)

                   Taxi   _____ (Receipt required)

                   Telephone   _____ (Detail on reverse)

                   Parking & Tolls   _____ (Receipt required)

                   Other Expenses   _____ (Detail on reverse)

                   Total Expenses $_____

                   Less Travel Advance   –_____

                   Total Due Employee
                   or Organization $_____ (Attach check)

Approved by: Name: _____

              Signature: _____

              Date: _____

For Accounting Use:

Account #	$ Amount	Account #	$ Amount
_____	_____	_____	_____
_____	_____	_____	_____
_____	_____	_____	_____

Monthly Expense Reimbursement Request

Date	Location Visited	Mileage	Other Expenses

TOTAL _____ $_____

Total Miles @ _____ ¢ per mile $_____

Total Other Expenses   _____

Total Requested $_____

Approved:

Name: _____   Name: _____

Signature: _____   Signature: _____

Date: _____   Date: _____

For Accounting Use:

Account #	$ Amount	Account #	$ Amount
_____	_____	_____	_____
_____	_____	_____	_____
_____	_____	_____	_____

| SUBJECT: | Unrelated Business Income Tax (UBIT) |

DISCUSSION:

Some revenue sources of tax-exempt organizations are subject to income taxes on the net profit of the activity if the revenue source is considered an activity unrelated to the tax exempt purpose of the organization. Briefly, current IRS regulations define an activity as unrelated if it possesses all three of the following criteria:

1. It is from a trade or business.

2. It is carried on regularly.

3. It is not substantially related to the organization's tax-exempt purpose.

The organization should have a policy whereby revenues and expenses for unrelated activities are clearly classified and designated in the financial records to stand up to IRS audit procedures. Revenues and expenses related to Unrelated Business Income Tax (UBIT) sources are reported on IRS Form 990-T.

SAMPLE POLICY:

It is the policy of the organization to pay UBIT on the excess of revenues over expenses on taxable activities. These activities will be clearly classified and designated in the financial records to provide adequate documentation in the event of an IRS audit.

The organization will file IRS Form 990-T to report unrelated activities. Form 990-T is considered confidential and is not available for public inspection.

See Form 990-T Policy in this manual.

SUBJECT:

Unrestricted Net Assets

DISCUSSION:

Unrestricted net assets are similar to retained earnings in commercial organizations in that they represent the cumulative results of operations of an organization. Unrestricted net assets represent the organization's net worth.

It is important to note and communicate to the board of directors that unrestricted net assets *include* board-designated funds and that unrestricted net assets are subject to creditor action. Proper financial statement presentation dictates that total unrestricted net assets, including board-designated funds, appear on the statement of financial position (balance sheet). It is acceptable to describe board-designated funds in footnotes or other supplemental information to the financial records, but board-designated funds have no legal or accounting significance.

SAMPLE POLICY:

It is the policy of the organization to include board-designated funds with unrestricted net assets on the Statement of Financial Position. A supplemental Statement of Board-Designated Funds Activity will be distributed with the financial statements.

See the Board-Designated Funds section of this manual.

SUBJECT: Voided Checks

DISCUSSION: Checks are voided for many reasons, such as errors made in the course
                                         of preparing a check, duplicate payments made to vendors, stop payments
                                         issued on lost checks, or stop payments issued because of disagreements
                                         with vendors.

                                         Regardless of the reason, it is essential that *every* voided check be
                                         accounted for and a voided checks log be maintained and available
                                         for the annual audit.

                                         Organizations should mark voided checks clearly with a "VOID" stamp,
                                         if the checks are physically available, and should file them in a voided
                                         checks file.

                                         If the physical check is not available (because it has been lost, for
                                         example), the organization's copy of the bank's stop-payment order
                                         should be filed in a stop-payment order file.

SAMPLE POLICY: It is the policy of the organization to maintain a Voided Checks Log
                                         and document every check that has been voided, regardless of the
                                         reason.

                                         If voided checks are physically available, they will be stamped "VOID"
                                         and filed in the organization's Voided Checks File.

                                         If voided checks are not physically available, the organization's copy
                                         of the bank's stop-payment order will be filed in a Stop-Payment
                                         Order File.

Voided Checks Log

Check #	Reason Check was Voided	Was Check Stamped "Void" and Filed? Yes / No	Was Stop-Payment Order Signed and Copy Filed? Yes / No

SUBJECT: Write-Off of Old Checks

DISCUSSION: The larger the organization, the more likely that a small number of checks processed will never be presented for payment and never clear the bank.

As part of its year-end procedures, an organization often writes off checks that have never cleared the bank if they are more than 12 months old. Assuming the amounts are relatively immaterial, it is common practice to increase available cash and credit miscellaneous revenue on the original expense account.

If a check of a material amount has failed to clear the bank, further contact with the payee is appropriate.

A log of written-off checks should be completed and made available for the annual audit.

SAMPLE POLICY: It is the policy of the organization to write off checks over 12 months old in conjunction with year-end procedures if the checks in question do not exceed $_____. When checks exceed this amount, contact with the payee will be initiated to resolve the issue. Written-off checks will be credited to miscellaneous revenue.

A Log of Written-Off Checks will be completed and made available for the annual audit.

Log of Written-Off Checks

Check #	Check Date	Check Amount	Payee
		$	

Glossary of Accounting and Financial Terminology

Accrual Accounting. Revenue is recognized when earned and expenses are recognized when incurred. Attempts to match revenue and expenses independently of cash receipts and disbursements.

Aged Statements. A report breaking down the accounts receivable and accounts payable schedules into monthly categories based on the original date of the invoice.

Amortization. Expensing an intangible or leasehold improvement over its useful life.

Assets. Economic resources, including cash, receivables, property, and intangibles.

Audit Exceptions. Problems incurred during the course of an audit by the independent CPA or the IRS.

Audited Financial Statements. Financial statements audited by an independent Certified Public Accountant (CPA) who has issued an accompanying opinion letter.

Balance Sheet. See *Statement of Financial Position.*

Board-Designated Funds. Amounts set aside by the board for a specific purpose but that have no legal or accounting significance. See *Unrestricted Net Assets.*

Book Value. The carrying value of an asset or liability, regardless of actual or market value. It is computed at cost less accumulated depreciation.

Capital Budgets. Projecting cash required to purchase fixed assets and resulting depreciation calculations.

Capital Lease. A lease that is recorded as an asset and depreciated rather than expensed on the financial records as payments are made.

Capitalization. Recording the cost of purchased assets on the organization's statement of financial position rather than expensing them in the period purchased. Capitalized assets are depreciated.

Cash Accounting. Revenue is recognized as cash is received, and expenses are recognized as cash is disbursed.

Cash Flow Budget. Projects cash-available balances at the end of each month to ensure sufficient cash is available to meet ongoing obligations and to maximize investment opportunities.

Continuous Budgeting. A process whereby monthly budgets are projected a year in advance every month after the current period financial statements are prepared.

Cost of Goods Sold. The actual cost of items sold to the organization that the organization intends to resell.

Credit. A credit entry will result in a reduction in an asset account, or an increase in a liability account, or a decrease in an expense account.

Current Assets. Cash plus cash equivalents plus assets that are expected to be converted to cash or consumed during the next 12 months.

Current Liabilities. Obligations due to be paid during the next 12 months.

Current Year Budget. Also called tactical plan. Organization's financial goals for the current year.

Debit. A debit entry will result in an increase in an asset account, or a reduction in a liability account, or an increase in an expense account.

Deferred Charges. Also known as prepaid expenses. An expenditure incurred in one period, the benefits from which are not realized until a later accounting period. It is recorded as an asset on the balance sheet.

Deferred Revenue. Revenue received before it is earned. It is recorded as a liability on the balance sheet.

Depreciation. Expensing a tangible asset over its economic life.

Endowment Funds. See *Permanently Restricted Net Assets.*

Expensing a Disbursement. Recording a disbursement of cash as an expense in the financial records rather than capitalizing the disbursement and recording it as an asset in the financial records.

Financial Ratios. Various computations to assess an organization's ability to pay debt, return on investment, and so forth.

Functional Accounting. Classifying revenues and expenses according to specific goals, departments, functions, and so forth.

Generally Accepted Accounting Principles (GAAP). A technical term encompassing conventions, rules, and procedures governing acceptable accounting practice.

Generally Accepted Auditing Standards (GAAS). Assumptions and rules that govern the CPA's ability to accept an auditing engagement and procedure that must be undertaken during the course of an audit.

Gross Revenues. The grand total of revenues received before deducting associated costs of goods sold and discounts taken.

Imprest Fund. Also known as petty cash fund. Cash kept on hand to pay for minor expenditures.

Income Statement. See *Statement of Activities.*

Intangible Asset. A nonfinancial asset to an organization with economic value. Examples include purchased copyrights with future royalty benefits, etc.

Internal Financial Statements. Unaudited financial statements used for management purposes only.

IRS Form 990. Information return required to be filed by not-for-profit organizations.

IRS Form 990–T. Tax return required to be filed by not-for-profit organizations for unrelated business income tax activities.

Leasehold Improvement. An expenditure that improves leased property, such as the purchase of office carpeting. The value of the improvement transfers to the owner of the property after the lease terminates.

Liabilities. Obligations to pay amounts or rend
of a past transaction.

Long-Range Plans. Also called strategic plans. Org
jected for five or more years.

Natural Accounting. Classifying expenses as line it
statements rather than classifying them according t

Net Assets. Section of the statement of financial positio   ...ues
unrestricted, temporarily restricted, and permanently restric...u net assets.

Net Revenues. Gross revenues less associated cost of goods sold and
discounts taken.

Net Worth. See Unrestricted Net Assets.

Operating Lease. An ongoing expense line item lease. Operating lease
expense is recognized on the financial statements as payments are made.

Permanently Restricted Net Assets. Endowment funds and other funds
that can only be used for activities stipulated by the donor.

Prepaid Expenses. Also known as deferred charges. An expenditure
incurred in one period, the benefits from which are not realized until
a later accounting period. It is recorded as an asset on the balance sheet.

Profit and Loss Statement. See *Statement of Activities*.

Quid pro quo Contribution. Contributions for which the donor receives
some value in return for the contribution.

Retirement of Assets. Removing the cost and accumulated depreciation
of an asset from the financial statements and records.

Statement of Activities. Revenues, expenses, and results of activities
of not-for-profit organizations. Called income statement or profit and
loss statement in commercial organizations.

Statement of Changes in Net Assets. Financial statement of a not-for-
profit organization indicating how results of operations have affected
unrestricted net assets (net worth of the not-for-profit), temporarily
restricted net assets, and permanently restricted net assets.

Statement of Financial Position. Assets, liabilities, and net assets of
a not-for-profit organization. Called balance sheet in commercial
organizations.

Temporarily Restricted Net Assets. Results of fundraising activities
for a specific purpose or project.

Unrelated Business Income Tax (UBIT). Tax paid on profits from
taxable activities. See *IRS Form 990–T.*

Unrestricted Net Assets. The net worth of a not-for-profit organization
including board-designated funds.

Zero-Based Budgeting. A process whereby actual historical financial
records are not used as a reference when budgets are prepared.

Index